yourself

beginner's turkish
asuman çelen pollard

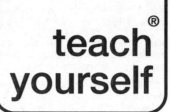

teach
yourself

beginner's turkish
asuman çelen pollard

For over 60 years, more than 40 million people have learnt over 750 subjects the **teach yourself** way, with impressive results.

be where you want to be with **teach yourself**

Dedication
for Vanessa-Su

For UK order enquiries: please contact Bookpoint Ltd, 130 Milton Park, Abingdon, Oxon OX14 4SB. Telephone: +44 (0) 1235 827720, Fax: +44 (0) 1235 400454. Lines are open 9.00–18.00, Monday to Saturday, with a 24-hour message answering service. Details about our titles and how to order are available at www.teachyourself.co.uk

For USA order enquiries: please contact McGraw-Hill Customer Services, P.O. Box 545, Blacklick, OH 43004-0545, USA. Telephone: 1-800-722-4726. Fax: 1-614-755-5645.

For Canada order enquiries: please contact McGraw-Hill Ryerson Ltd, 300 Water St, Whitby, Ontario L1N 9B6, Canada. Telephone: 905 430 5000. Fax: 905 430 5020.

Long renowned as the authoritative source for self-guided learning – with more than 30 million copies sold worldwide – the *Teach Yourself* series includes over 300 titles in the fields of languages, crafts, hobbies, business, computing and education.

British Library Cataloguing in Publication Data
A catalogue entry for this title is available from The British Library.

Library of Congress Catalog Card Number: on file.

First published in UK 2003 by Hodder Headline Ltd, 338 Euston Road, London, NW1 3BH.

First published in US 2003 by Contemporary Books, a division of The McGraw-Hill Companies, 1 Prudential Plaza, 130 East Randolph Street, Chicago, Illinois 60601 USA.

The 'Teach Yourself' name is a registered trade mark of Hodder & Stoughton Ltd.

Copyright © 2003 Asuman Çelen Pollard

Typeset by Transet Limited, Coventry, England.
Printed in Great Britain for Hodder & Stoughton Educational, a division of Hodder Headline Ltd, 338 Euston Road, London NW1 3BH by Cox & Wyman Ltd, Reading, Berkshire.

Impression number   10 9 8 7 6 5 4 3 2 1
Year   2008 2007 2006 2005 2004 2003

v2

contents

introduction		vii
	how to use this book	viii
	why learn about Turkish culture?	ix
	learning tips	x
	the alphabet and pronunciation	xi
01	**greetings**	**1**

saying 'hello', 'goodbye' and 'how are you?'
• learning about Turkish names; Mr, Mrs, Ms
• numbers 1–10 • pronunciation: *a, b, c*

02	**drinks**	**10**

ordering drinks • calling the waiter • asking
for the bill • numbers to 100 • ordering snacks
• colours • pronunciation: *ç, d, e*

03	**accommodation**	**21**

enquiring about accommodation • choosing
somewhere to stay • asking about the facilities
• checking in • filling in forms • numbers –
hundreds and thousands • telephone numbers
• pronunciation: *f, g, ğ*

04	**eating out**	**35**

ordering meals • enquiring what dishes there
are and what's in them • how to pay the bill
• pronunciation: *h, ı, i*

05	**directions**	**48**

asking for and giving directions • getting
around a new place • asking what something
means • pronunciation: *j, k, l*

06   **I like the weather here!**   **63**
      talking about the weather • comparing months
      and seasons • talking about your likes and
      dislikes • pronunciation: *m, n, o*

07   **talking about oneself and describing
      people**   **80**
      talking about yourself (I am …) • asking
      people about themselves (are you…?)
      • describing yourself and other people
      • pronunciation: *ö, p, r*

08   **shopping**   **96**
      shopping for presents and clothes • talking
      about what is happening (-iyor)
      • pronunciation: *s, ş, t*

09   **where shall we go?**   **111**
      making arrangements to go out • suggesting
      doing something (let's, shall we) • telling the
      time • booking seats at the theatre • buying
      tickets for public transport • pronunciation:
      u, ü, v

10   **how was it?**   **129**
      talking about the past, including your
      experiences and historical facts • writing a
      postcard • having a social chat
      • pronunciation: *y, z*

taking it further   **145**
translations   **147**
transcripts   **162**
key to the exercises   **171**
glossary of grammatical terms   **180**
appendix: vowel harmony   **184**
Turkish–English vocabulary   **185**
English–Turkish vocabulary   **197**
index   **207**

Welcome to *Teach Yourself Beginner's Turkish*. This course is for anyone who wants to speak and write some basic Turkish so that they can get the most out of a visit to Turkey.

Starting with the alphabet and pronunciation, we have designed the units so that your Turkish builds gradually. We have included topics and situations which visitors to Turkey will find immediately useful. There are ten carefully graded and interlocking units.

We have assumed no previous knowledge of foreign language learning and have avoided grammatical terminology where possible. Since the book is aimed at beginners, we have tried to keep the language points and explanations as simple and straightforward as possible. The Turkish language works very differently from English, and some letters of the alphabet look different from English – but do not be put off by this. The good news is that Turkish, unlike English, is very logical and regular. With some basic knowledge, you will quickly be able to read and speak Turkish. We have focussed on Turkish as spoken in Istanbul at the turn of the 21st century.

This book is intended for you to use on your own, with the support of the accompanying recordings, indicated by ▶ in your book. It can also be used for study with a teacher. Each unit contains dialogues, which are all recorded and have (natural) English translations at the back of the book, language and culture points, with plenty of examples, and all the necessary vocabulary. At the end of each unit, there are exercises for practice, including occasionally wordsearches to reinforce the vocabulary, and a mini-test which is also recorded, for you to check your progress. At the back of the book, you will find the answer key for the exercises and a glossary, as well as the dialogue translations.

How to use this book

As modern Turkish is a phonetic language we have started with the Turkish alphabet and pronunciation. Look at the letters, listen to them more than once, then imitate the sounds. At this stage do not try to learn the alphabet by heart. Once you have practised it you can refer back to it if you need to. Throughout the book there is plenty of pronunciation practice. Unit 3 concentrates on the alphabet and Turkish names to give more practice.

Each unit has at least two dialogues. Most of the dialogues have very simple comprehension questions before and after. The mini-test and exercises are essential parts of each unit. For each unit you can choose whether you read each dialogue first or listen to it first. You may prefer to do both together. Whichever way you do it, listen to and read the dialogues a number of times.

Do not worry if you don't understand everything, your understanding will improve as time goes on. Don't try to learn all the items in the vocabulary box off by heart – you can go back any time you want. In real life, people do not learn lists of vocabulary – they are simply exposed to words over and over again in a context which they know, and in the end (with a little looking-up or asking) things stick.

Speak along with the dialogues as you get to know them and imitate what you hear. Don't be afraid to make mistakes.

After checking your understanding with the comprehension questions and answers, read the language points carefully and go back to the dialogue.

The practice exercises are where you can have some fun. If you want to write the answers in the book, do so in pencil. Then you can rub them out later and try again. When you have completed a couple of units, go back to the exercises in earlier units – it is very satisfying to find them easier to do than the first time!

Early on in your studies find something real to read, such as Turkish newspapers, magazines or comics. If you have access to the internet spend a few moments searching for items in Turkish – you may turn up anything from a collection of Turkish recipes to the life story of Ataturk. We have put some web addresses of general interest at the back of the book and some units have references to websites related specifically to the content of the unit.

Set yourself a routine for learning, somewhere relaxed. Look at our section called **Learning tips**. You may find some of the advice helpful, especially if you are returning to learning after a long break.

A note about Turkish money

Inflation in Turkey is very high – over 50% in some years. This has two main implications for students of Turkish: one is that any prices quoted in course books will quickly be out of date, the other is that students need to learn large numbers to do even basic shopping. At the time of writing, there are nearly 3 million Turkish lira to the pound sterling. You need to be able to express hundreds of thousands to buy drinks and snacks.

Why learn about Turkish culture?

Throughout the book, we have included culture notes (marked with ⓘ in the book) alongside language learning points. We have done this for a number of reasons. People from different cultures use language in different ways and as you start to learn Turkish a little knowledge of the cultural context will help you communicate well with Turkish people. Good communication is not always about accurate pronunciation and grammar – if you learn the manners and customs expected by native speakers of a language, you will be received with friendship and respect. Also knowing about the culture of a country you visit helps you understand what you see and hear around you. For example, if you listen to English speakers shopping in England you will hear them using 'please' and 'thank you' many times. This would seem a little strange to Turkish speakers, who express politeness differently – in the way they greet the shopkeeper and the form of address they express through verb endings.

Philosophers argue whether the way a language works reflects the thinking of its speakers, or vice versa! This argument has a chicken and egg feel and is hard to resolve, but it is interesting to note that whilst English speakers wish each other just one 'Good night', Turkish speakers wish each other **İyi geceler** (many 'Good nights')! Hospitality, good manners and respectful social interaction are very important in Turkish culture. Turkish has set phrases to wish people well on a wide range of occasions, such as when offering and receiving food, getting a haircut and wearing new clothes. If you learn to use a few of these, Turkish speakers will be delighted by your manners.

We hope you will find the culture notes interesting, as well as useful preparation for a visit to Turkey.

Life after this book

Once you have completed this book, you will be able to communicate in a variety of everyday situations and have a sound knowledge of the basic Turkish language points. What then? You can move to *Teach Yourself Turkish*.

Enjoy your learning!

Symbols

▶ This indicates that the recording is needed.

ℹ Cultural information.

Learning tips

This book is for all kinds of people learning Turkish, for a wide range of reasons. This may be the first time you have tried to learn another language. We have planned the units to build up your Turkish gently, step by step – but once you have started, you may want to explore the book at your own pace. One of the advantages of a self-study book like this is that you can return to a section as many times as you need, working at your own speed.

Here are some tips on language learning that you may find helpful in getting the most out of this book:

1 **Be active in your learning.** Find out which ways of learning work for you. Everyone is different.
2 **Do a little bit every day.** Don't expect to be able to learn large amounts in one sitting. Set yourself a goal of learning a certain number of new words every day, say 5–10.
3 **Create learning habits.** Set time aside for your learning on a regular basis. Stick to a routine.
4 **Don't wait till you can speak the language perfectly – speak to yourself!**
5 **Be positive about your achievements.** Enjoy learning. Concentrate on what you have learnt, not on what you cannot remember.

6 **Get a good dictionary.** When you come across a new word, try to guess the meaning first, then use a good dictionary to check. If you want to learn the word, write it down, with the definition and the word in context.

7 **Create your own personal vocabulary book.** Group the words either in grammar type (e.g. separate sections for verbs, nouns and adjectives), or by theme (e.g. food, drink, transport, numbers), or according to the purpose they serve in conversation (e.g. how to greet people / how to shop / how to order a meal).

8 **Don't worry too much about making mistakes.** Mistakes are a natural part of learning. Turkish speakers will be pleased that you are having a go and will appreciate anything you can say.

9 **Revise regularly.** Use the mini-test at the end of each unit.

10 **Listen carefully.** Listen to the recording, or if possible a native speaker or a teacher, repeating out loud whenever possible. If you can, get some help from a Turkish speaker or find out about Turkish clubs or societies in your area.

11 **Record yourself.** Record yourself and compare your pronunciation with a native speaker, then try again.

12 **Make flashcards.** Write the Turkish words you are trying to learn on small cards and stick them around the house where you will come across them during the day. Relevant pictures could be an extra support for word meanings.

13 **Don't give up.** Keep going, using little treats or rewards for your achievements along the way to keep up your motivation. Enjoy it.

BOL ŞANSLAR!

The alphabet and pronunciation

The Latin alphabet was adopted by the Republic of Turkey in 1928. Prior to that, Turkish was written in Arabic script. Nowadays, Turkish uses the Latin script, with a small number of modifications. It has 29 letters: eight of them (a, ı, o, u, e, i, ö, ü) are vowels, the remaining 21 are consonants. Some vowels differ from English sounds but English speakers can pronounce all of the sounds with little difficulty. Once you have learnt the alphabet, you will find Turkish simple and straightforward to read, because unlike English

- you pronounce Turkish in exactly the same way as you spell it
- each Turkish letter stands for a single sound.

Here is the Turkish alphabet. This book focuses on Turkish as spoken in Istanbul at the turn of the 21st century, which is Standard Turkish.

▶ Listen to the alphabet while looking at the following list of sounds, then repeat the sounds out loud as you hear them.

Turkish letter	Letter name pronounced roughly as English	Sound pronounced roughly as English
Aa	*ah*	*a*rt
Bb	*bay*	*b*ig
Cc	*jay*	*J*ohn
Çç	*chay*	*ch*ild
Dd	*dey*	*d*o
Ee	*ey*	g*e*t
Ff	*fey*	*f*ar
Gg	*gay*	*g*et
Ğğ yumuşak ğ	*yumushak gay*	this letter has no sound!
Hh	*hey*	*h*ow
Iı	*uh*	butt*e*r
İi	*ee*	*i*t
Jj	*zhe*	plea*s*ure
Kk	*kay*	*k*itten
Ll	*ley*	*l*ovely
Mm	*mey*	*m*an
Nn	*ney*	*n*o
Oo	*o*	b*o*x
Öö	*ur*	d*i*rt
Pp	*pay*	*p*en
Rr	*ray*	d*r*y
Ss	*say*	*s*ea
Şş	*shay*	*sh*ow
Tt	*tay*	*t*ea
Uu	*oo*	p*u*ll
Üü	*ew*	German *ü* or French *tu*
Vv	*vey*	*v*ery
Yy	*ye*	*y*es
Zz	*zey*	*z*ip

Note the difference between İ or i with a dot and I or ı without a dot.

In English we do not always pronounce every letter. Turkish is different – you always pronounce all the letters. What you see is what you say! The only slight exception is the letter ğ. The letter ğ is called **yumuşak g**, which means *soft g*. It always comes after a vowel and turns that vowel into a long sound. You might think of it as doubling the vowel before it. Therefore, think of **ağ** as *aa* or think of **öğle** as *ööle*. There are no words beginning with **g** soft (ğ).

▶ Now it's your turn to practise

Listen to the following 29 letters of the Turkish alphabet and repeat the example words out loud as you hear them. They are all towns and cities in Turkey, except one. Listen for the odd one out!

A	Ankara	M	Malatya
B	Bursa	N	Niğde
C	Ceyhan	O	Ordu
Ç	Çanakkale	Ö	Ödemiş
D	Denizli	P	Perşembe
E	Edirne	R	Rize
F	Fatsa	S	Samsun
G	Giresun	Ş	Şırnak
Ğ	*yumuşak G*	T	Tokat
H	Hatay	U	Urfa
I	Isparta	Ü	Üsküdar
İ	İzmir	V	Van
J	Japonya	Y	Yozgat
K	Konya	Z	Zonguldak
L	Lüleburgaz		

For more practice turn to Unit 3. Now you have learnt the sounds of Turkish you can read a newspaper even if you cannot understand it! But at this stage, knowing your sounds and letters will be very useful if you need to look at a menu or phrase book.

Acknowledgements

Special thanks to Paul Warren for his IT skills. I would not have been able even to start without his support and encouragement. I feel I'm in debt to him forever.

I would like to thank my student, my friend, my English consultant and assistant writer Trisha Wick for working and being alongside me from the beginning and for adding sparkles. And also my student Dr Cymone Argent for being my English consultant and for being so perceptive and meticulous. And my dear sister Ülkü Çelen Gezer for being my eyes and ears in Turkey.

Also thank you for contributions from: Aliye Uçar, Lesley Campbell, Anne England, A.Yeşim Gökşin, Gül Melhuish and, of course, Vanessa-Su.

And last but not least, I would like to thank all the people at Hodder and Stoughton, especially my editors, for being so supportive. Their professional contribution has been priceless.

01

greetings

In this unit you will learn
- how to say 'hello!'
- how to say 'goodbye!'
- how to say 'how are you?'
- Mr, Mrs, Ms
- numbers (1–10)
- pronunciation: a, b, c

Dialogues

First listen to the dialogues on the recording without looking at the book. Then listen again whilst reading them. Then listen and read the dialogue, pause the recording after each word and sentence and repeat out loud. Don't worry, just relax and try to copy what you hear. Keep practising till you know the words almost by heart.

Look up any words you don't know in the vocabulary box. See if you can understand the conversation for yourself. If you need more help, you can find translations of all the dialogues at the back of the book.

▶ Dialogue 1 Good evening

Ülkü, Doktor Bahadır Bey, Hüseyin and Banu are all at a party in a club. Ülkü is married to Bahadır, who joins them later. He is in his forties. Hüseyin approaches Ülkü and introduces himself.

Hüseyin İyi akşamlar, ben Hüseyin. Ya, siz?
Ülkü İyi akşamlar, ben Ülkü.
Hüseyin Nasılsınız, Ülkü Hanım?
Ülkü Teşekkürler, Hüseyin Bey. İyiyim. Siz nasılsınız?
Hüseyin Ben de iyiyim.
They shake hands. Hüseyin offers Ülkü a glass of wine. She accepts.
Hüseyin Şarap?
Ülkü Evet, lütfen.

Question
Answer the following question based on the dialogue, then check your answer in the back of the book.

Hüseyin hanım mı?

iyi	good
iyi akşamlar	good evening
ben	I
ya, siz? / ya sen?	and you?
nasılsınız? / nasılsın?	how are you?
Hanım	Miss / Mrs (after the first name only)
teşekkürler	thanks
Bey	Mr (after the first name only)
iyiyim	I am fine
siz / sen	you
ben de	me too (lit. I too)
şarap	wine
evet	yes
lütfen	please

▶ Dialogue 2 Hi, how are you?
Then Ülkü's husband joins them.

Bahadır Merhaba Ülkü, nasılsın?
Ülkü İyiyim, teşekkürler. Sen nasılsın?
Bahadır Ben de iyiyim. (*They kiss each other on both cheeks.*)
Ülkü offers Bahadır a beer. He accepts.
Ülkü Bira?
Bahadır Evet, lütfen.

Questions
1 Ülkü nasıl?
2 Bahadır nasıl?

merhaba / selam	hello / hi	bira	beer

▶ Dialogue 3 It's a very nice party
Ülkü introduces herself to Banu, who is 26 years old. Later on Bahadır joins the conversation. Banu has to leave quite early.

Ülkü	İyi akşamlar, ben Ülkü. Ya, sen?
Banu	İyi akşamlar, ben Banu. (*They shake hands.*)
Ülkü	Nasılsın, Banu?
Banu	(*Smiles.*) Teşekkürler, iyiyim.
Ülkü	Çok güzel bir parti, değil mi?
Banu	Evet, çok güzel.
Ülkü	Banu, Dr Bahadır Bey. (*They shake hands.*)

Question

Parti nasıl?

çok	*very*
güzel	*beautiful, nice*
bir	*a* (see explanation, page 6)
parti	*party*
değil	*not*
değil mi?	*isn't it?*

▶ Dialogue 4 Goodbye

Bahadır joins them.

Bahadır	İyi akşamlar.
Banu	İyi akşamlar, Bahadır Bey.
Bahadır	Nasılsın, Banu?
Banu	Teşekkürler, iyiyim. Siz nasılsınız?
Bahadır	Ben de iyiyim.

Banu looks at her watch as she has to leave early. She says goodbye to Ülkü and Bahadır, and wishes everybody goodnight.

Banu	Hoşça kalın, Ülkü Hanım. Hoşça kalın, Bahadır Bey. İyi geceler.
Ülkü and Bahadır	Güle güle, Banu.

Question

Banu nasıl?

Listen to the words in the dialogue while looking at their spelling. Repeat the words out loud as you hear them. Relax and enjoy speaking Turkish!

hoşça kalın	*goodbye*
iyi geceler	*good night*
güle güle	*goodbye* (reply to **hoşça kalın**)

Language points

Using *sen* or *siz* (you)

You probably noticed that Ülkü changed the form of her language slightly in each dialogue, although she meant the same thing.

Turkish has two ways of saying *you*, depending on how well you know the other person. **Sen** means *you* when you are speaking to one person whom you know well. So in the second dialogue Ülkü asked her husband, 'Sen nasılsın?'

If you are speaking to one person whom you do not know, **siz** means *you*. So when meeting Hüseyin for the first time, Ülkü asked, 'Siz, nasılsınız?' When you use **siz**, **nasılsın** changes to **nasılsınız**. You would also use the **siz** form to show respect to someone who is older than you, or of a higher social standing than you, such as your boss. If you use **siz** when speaking to someone, they will think you are polite and respectful – so if in doubt, use **siz**!

Siz also always means *you* when you are speaking to more than one person, even if you know them very well.

If you are familiar with French, you'll notice that **sen** and **siz** work like *tu* and *vous*.

Names

In Turkey, surnames are not used when greeting people. If you want to be polite, you use the person's first name with **Hanım** for a woman, and **Bey** for a man. Ülkü and Hüseyin are being courteous on first meeting, so Ülkü said, '**Teşekkürler, Hüseyin Bey**', and Hüseyin referred to her as '**Ülkü Hanım**'. People's first names are used without **Hanım** or **Bey** only if you know them well and you are roughly the same age.

değil means 'not'

To make a word or phrase negative, e.g. *it's not*, place **değil** after the word or phrase.

Şarap değil.   *It's not wine.*

Değil mi? changes a word or a phrase into the question, *isn't it* or *aren't they?*

Şarap, *değil mi?*   *Wine, isn't it?*
Çok güzel bir parti,   *A very good party, isn't it?*
  değil mi?

bir sometimes means 'a'

In Turkish there is no word that means *a* or *the*. Sometimes **bir**, which means *one*, is used to mean *a* or *an*:

Bir parti   *a party*

❶ Kissing and shaking hands

In Turkey, social kissing on both cheeks is common between people of the same sex. Young, westernized Turks shake hands when greeting each other and kiss on both cheeks. Strict Moslems do **not** kiss and shake hands with the opposite sex, only with the same sex. Kissing in public between lovers is not socially acceptable.

❶ 00

Have you ever noticed **00** on a door in Turkey and wondered what it meant? It simply means *toilet*! So learning your numbers may just come in very handy next time you are in Turkey. (We'll tell you more about asking for the toilet later in the book – hope you can wait!)

▶ Saying 'hello'

First listen to, then repeat the phrases. After that write them down and practise until you feel you have learnt them. Do not forget to revise them at regular intervals.

Günaydın (7 a.m. to midday)	İyi akşamlar (5 p.m. to 10 p.m.)	İyi geceler (After 10 p.m.)

In the afternoon Turkish people usually use **merhaba**; however in more formal situations, such as talking to their boss, they would use **iyi günler**.

▶ Numbers

First read and listen to these numbers; then pause the recording and repeat each number after the speaker. Do this many times until you feel comfortable with all the numbers. When you feel confident, test yourself. Try saying the numbers from 0 to 10 without looking at the book. Then try saying them backwards, from 10 to 0.

0	**sıfır**	6	**altı**
1	**bir**	7	**yedi**
2	**iki**	8	**sekiz**
3	**üç**	9	**dokuz**
4	**dört**	10	**on**
5	**beş**		

Practice

1 How would you say 'Hello' to the following people at the time shown?

More than one answer is possible.

a To your friends.

b To your grandmother.

c To your boss.

2 It is late at night and you decide to go to bed. What would you say to your Turkish friends?

3 How would you say 'Goodbye' to your Turkish host?

4 What would the response be?

5 Fill in the blanks.

a M_ _ _ _ _ _, ben Şafak.

b Selam, _ _ _ Gökhan.

6 Reorder the following sentences to make a dialogue. Start with the phrase in bold. (The dialogue is between two friends.)

a Hoşça kal.
b İyiyim, sen nasılsın?
c Merhaba Gülen, nasılsın?
d Ben de iyiyim.
e **Merhaba, Ali.**
f Güle güle.

7 Write down the following numbers as figures.

a beş	e üç	i altı
b on	f yedi	j sekiz
c bir	g dört	k sıfır
d dokuz	h iki	

8 Do these sums:

a dört + üç =	f dört – iki =
b bir + bir =	g beş – iki =
c üç + üç =	h on – bir =
d dört + beş =	i dokuz – bir =
e iki + altı =	

▶ **9** In each unit you will get the opportunity to practise your pronunciation. **Pronunciation: a, b, c.** First, listen without looking, second, listen while looking, finally listen and repeat.

a	b	c
aaa	ba ba	can
aç	beş	ece
ad	bir	öc
af	bira	acı

10 Look at the wordsearch. There are ten words which you have learnt. Can you find them? One has been found for you.

M	E	R	H	A	B	A	B	İ	R
N	R	S	A	V	E	Z	A	K	T
A	C	İ	N	O	Y	D	O	İ	R
S	L	A	I	N	P	J	S	T	V
I	R	C	M	P	O	U	S	E	N
L	F	N	O	P	Z	H	İ	B	J
S	A	L	T	İ	R	S	Z	J	C
I	B	N	T	R	P	S	O	V	J
N	İ	Y	İ	Y	İ	M	R	T	U
P	S	I	R	G	D	Ç	F	O	N

▶ Mini-test

Well done! You have reached the end of Unit 1. Let's see what you can remember. Give yourself a point if you can say the following in Turkish without looking at the **Key to the exercises**.

1 How do you say 'hello'?
2 How do you say 'goodbye'?
3 How do you say 'goodnight'?
4 How do you ask your boss how she is?
5 How do you ask your friend how he is?
6 How do you say 'thank you'?
7 Recite the Turkish alphabet.
8 How do you say the numbers 1–10?
9 How do you introduce yourself?
10 How do you say, 'I'm fine, thank you. How are you?'

Points:_____/10

If you get any wrong, go back through the unit and have another look before moving on to the next unit.

02

drinks

In this unit you will learn
- how to order drinks
- how to call the waiter
- how to ask for the bill
- numbers 10–100
- how to order snacks
- basic colours
- pronunciation: c, d, e

◘ Dialogue 1 A glass of tea, please

Banu and Şafak are cousins. They are sitting at a table in a café in Istanbul by the Bosporus. A waiter comes to take the order.

Garson	Buyrun, efendim?
Banu	Bir bardak çay, lütfen.

The waiter writes down the order and repeats it to check he has written it down correctly.

Garson	Bir bardak çay. (*The waiter turns to Şafak.*) Siz, efendim?
Şafak	Bir bira ve bir şişe su, lütfen.
Garson	Bira yok, efendim.
Şafak	İçecek ne var?

The waiter hands Şafak a menu.

Garson	Buyrun, mönü.

Şafak looks at the menu.

Şafak	Teşekkür. Bir Nescafé, lütfen.
Garson	Süt?
Şafak	Evet, sütlü.

The waiter writes down the order and repeats it out loud to check that he has written it down correctly.

Garson	Bir çay, bir sütlü Nescafé.
Şafak	Evet, tamam.

The waiter comes back and puts the drinks on the table.

Garson	Bir çay, bir Nescafé, şeker, süt.
Banu and Şafak	Teşekkürler.
Garson	Afiyet olsun, efendim.

Şafak calls the waiter and asks for the bill.

Şafak	Garson!
Garson	Buyrun.
Şafak	Hesap, lütfen.

They pay the bill and tell the waiter to keep the change (it is usual to leave a 10% tip at cafés and restaurants).

Şafak	Üstü kalsın.
Garson	Sağ olun, efendim.

Questions

1 İçecek ne var?
2 Nescafé nasıl?

Buyrun*, efendim?	*How can I help you, sir / madam?*
bardak	*glass*
çay	*tea*
şişe	*bottle*
yok	*there is none / we haven't got any*
içecek	*drink*
ne	*what*
var	*there is / are*
mönü	*menu*
teşekkür	*thank you* (alternative to **teşekkürler**)
Nescafé	*instant coffee*
süt	*milk*
sütlü	*with milk*
tamam	*OK*
şeker	*sugar*
afiyet olsun	*enjoy your drinks! / enjoy your meal!*
garson	*waiter! / waitress!*
buyrun*	*yes, sir*
hesap	*the bill*
üstü kalsın	*keep the change*
sağ olun	*thanks* (showing respect and gratitude)

***Buyurun** is the correct dictionary spelling. **Buyrun** is what people say.

Language points

bir: 'a' or 'one'

The Turkish word **bir** is very useful. It means the number *one*, but it can also mean *a* as in *a bottle of beer* (**bir şişe bira**).

▶ More numbers

First read and listen to the following numbers, then pause the recording and repeat each number after the speaker. When you feel confident test yourself. To say more numbers, just put the words together: 41 = **kırkbir**. Now try saying the numbers from 10 to 20 and then the multiples of ten up to 100 without looking at the book. Next try saying them backwards.

10	**on**	18	**on sekiz**
11	**on bir**	19	**on dokuz**
12	**on iki**	20	**yirmi**
13	**on üç**	30	**otuz**
14	**on dört**	40	**kırk**
15	**on beş**	50	**elli**
16	**on altı**	60	**altmış**
17	**on yedi**	70	**yetmiş**

80 seksen
90 doksan
100 yüz

Note: In English we say *one hundred*. In Turkish you just say **yüz**.

▶ Dialogue 2 The coffee is very good here

Turkish restaurants and cafés make children very welcome. A family is seen sitting at the next table to Banu and Şafak. They are enjoying a day out together. The waiter approaches their table and they order some drinks.

Garson	Buyrun, efendim.
Mother	Bir şekerli kahve.
Father	Bana da, şekersiz.

The mother asks the child what she would like.

Mother Sen yavrum? Limonata?

The child looks at the menu.

Child Hayır, ayran.
Mother Tamam.

The father orders for everyone and the waiter writes it down.

Father İki kahve, bir şekerli, bir sade ve bir ayran.
Garson Tabii, efendim.

Bir fincan kahve

The waiter brings the drinks, which include two glasses of water to go with the coffees (Turkish coffee is usually served with a glass of water).

Garson Buyrun efendim, içecekleriniz.
Everyone Teşekkürler.
Garson Afiyet olsun.
Mother Kahveler çok güzel, değil mi?
Father Evet, çok güzel.
Child Acıktım.
Mother Ben de. Tost?
Child Evet, peynirli tost ve ayran.

The father calls the waiter and gives him the order.

Father Garson, lütfen.
Garson Buyrun?
Father Üç peynirli tost ve üç ayran lütfen.

While waiting for the food, the mother enjoys the view.

Mother Manzara çok güzel, değil mi?
Father Evet, çok güzel.

Questions

1 Kahveler nasıl?
2 Manzara güzel, değil mi?

şekerli	*sweet*
bana da	*for me too*
şekersiz	*without sugar*
yavrum	*my child* (shows affection)
limonata	*still lemonade*
ayran	*ayran* (yoghurt-based drink)
sade	*without sugar*
içecekleriniz	*your drinks*
afiyet olsun	*enjoy your drinks*
acıktım	*I'm hungry*
tost	*toasted sandwich*
peynirli tost	*toasted cheese sandwich*
manzara	*view*

Language points

Ordering drinks in Turkish is very easy – all you need to know are your numbers and the name of the drinks! Unlike in English, you don't change the ending of the name of the drink when ordering more than one. So *two teas* is **iki çay**. *Three beers* is **üç bira** and so on. The most difficult part is choosing what you want!

Plurals (more than one)

Singular	Plural
akşam	akşamlar
kahve	kahveler
tost	tostlar

In Turkish all nouns (names of things, opinions and feelings, etc.) can be made plural by adding **-ler** or **-lar**. For example, **akşam** (*evening*) becomes **akşamlar** (*evenings*). Unlike English, however, Turkish has no irregular forms. The good news is you only need to learn one rule, and you can make any Turkish noun plural. You put **-lar** if the last vowel is one of these letters: **a, ı, o, u; -ler** if the last vowel is one of these: **e, i, ö, ü**. This follows one of the rules of vowel harmony. We call this formation of the plural an 'e-type' ending.

In Turkish most salutations are in the plural. Here are some examples.

iyi akşamlar	*good evening*
iyi geceler	*goodnight*
selamlar	*hello*
tebrikler	*congratulations*
mutlu yıllar	*happy new year*
mutlu bayramlar	*have a happy Bayram* (see Unit 9)
iyi şanslar	*good luck*
iyi yolculuklar	*have a good journey*
iyi günler	*good day*
renkli rüyalar	*sweet dreams*

▶ Dialogue 3 One red wine, please

Banu and Şafak meet in a bar later the same day.

Şafak	İyi akşamlar.
Garson	İyi akşamlar, efendim. Buyrun?
Banu	Bir şarap, lütfen.
Şafak	Kırmızı mı, beyaz mı?
Banu	Kırmızı, lütfen.
Şafak	Bir kırmızı şarap ve bir rakı lütfen.
Garson	Tabii, efendim. Çerez?
Şafak	Evet, fıstık, biraz da karışık meyve ve beyaz peynir, lütfen.
Garson	Tabii, efendim.

Questions

1 Şarap ne renk?
2 Beyaz peynir mi?

şarap	*wine*
kırmızı	*red*
kırmızı mı?	*red?*
beyaz	*white*
beyaz mı?	*white?*
ve	*and*
rakı	*raki (aniseed-flavoured spirit)*
çerez	*snacks*
fıstık	*nuts*
biraz da	*and (some) also*
karışık	*mixed*
meyve	*fruit*
peynir	*cheese*

Language points

▶ Renkler *Colours*

beyaz	*white*	**pembe**	*pink*
kırmızı	*red*	**siyah**	*black*
mavi	*blue*	**gri**	*grey*
yeşil	*green*	**mor**	*purple*
sarı	*yellow*	**turuncu**	*orange*

Can you work out what these combinations mean?

- **kahverengi**
- **şaraprengi**
- **turkuaz mavi**

Check in the Vocabulary list at the back of the book to see if you are right!

Asking questions

Did you notice that the mother and the waiter turned the name of a drink into a question? E.g. **Limonata? Çerez?** This would probably sound a bit abrupt in English, but is perfectly normal in Turkish. Listen again! The mother asks her daughter if she would like some lemonade by simply saying **Limonata?**, and raising the pitch of her voice at the end of the word. This is a really easy way of making a question, isn't it. Have a go!

var and yok *there is/are/not*

Var means *there is* or *there are*.

Ne var?	*What's there? / What have you got?*
Çay var.	*There is tea.*
Rakı var.	*There is raki.*

Yok means *there isn't* or *there aren't (any).*

Ne yok?	*What isn't there? / What haven't you got?*
Kahve yok.	*There isn't any coffee.*
Bira yok	*There isn't any beer.*

🔢 Having a drink

Now you have learnt how to order a drink in a café, restaurant or bar. You are still left with the most difficult part: choosing what you want! All the usual European drinks are available such as beer, cola, spirits, wine, mineral water and fruit juices. However, you'll be missing out if you don't try some of the typically Turkish drinks such as **rakı** (a strong aniseed spirit usually diluted with water), **vişne suyu** *sour cherry juice*, **ayran** (a yoghurt drink), **çay** *tea* and **Türk kahvesi** *Turkish coffee*. **Çay** is served black in a tulip-shaped glass usually with sugar lumps on a saucer. The colour of the tea is all-important, as it is a guide to its quality. **Türk kahvesi** is also served black but in a small fine china cup, slightly smaller than an expresso one. Sugar, if required, is added during the making of coffee so you will need to learn the words to order coffee with sugar (**şekerli**), without sugar (**sade**) or with a little sugar (**az şekerli**). The coffee and sugar, if required, are heated up in a **cezve** (a small pot with a long handle) on a cooker. If you want an instant coffee, you need to ask for Nescafé. The preparation of both tea and coffee are real art forms.

Rakı, when mixed with water, goes white and is known as **Arslan Sütü** *lion's milk* because of its strength and colour. When **rakı** is ordered in a bar it is usually served with **beyaz peynir** *white cheese*, **zeytin** *olives* and **fıstık** *nuts*.

Practice

1 What is the Turkish for the following drinks?

a   b   c

d   e

▶ 2 Offer someone a drink by turning the names of the following drinks into questions by raising the tone of your voice at the end of the word. Listen to the recording to check you're right.

Example Şarap?

a   b   c

d   e

▶ **3** Make the following words plural by giving them -**ler** or -**lar** endings as appropriate. Listen to the recording first, then write down the answers

Example bardak → bardak**lar**.

a çay   d teşekkür
b rakı   e bira
c tost   f içecek

4 Write down what colour the following colour mixes make.

a mavi + sarı =   d beyaz + kırmızı =
b kırmızı + sarı =   e kırmızı + mavi =
c siyah + beyaz =

▶ **5 Pronunciation: ç, d, e.** First, listen without looking, then listen while looking and finally listen and repeat.

ç	d	e
çay	ad	ev
aç	de	ve
kaç	idi	et
açı	dün	kek

6 Look at the following sums. Put a tick next to those that are right (**doğru**) or a cross next to those that are wrong (**yanlış**).

                               doğru   yanlış
a on + yirmi = kırk
b otuz + elli = altmış
c on beş + on beş = otuz
d seksen – kırk = kırk
e yetmiş – elli = on

7 Write the following numbers in figures.

a sıfır   e yirmi üç
b elli yedi   f kırk altı
c on bir   g altmış
d otuz beş

8 Wordsearch. Find nine drinks hidden in this wordsearch. One has been done for you.

K	A	H	V	E	Ü	J	O	C	B
R	V	A	F	Ş	E	H	Ç	T	İ
Ç	P	S	Ü	T	B	T	J	Ü	R
V	İ	Ş	N	E	S	U	Y	U	A
E	K	A	C	S	U	İ	Y	R	S
Ş	N	Y	D	R	S	J	K	I	Y
A	H	R	N	Ç	B	R	A	K	I
R	E	A	S	T	O	V	A	K	Y
A	K	N	O	A	Ü	Ş	I	T	Ü
P	E	Ç	A	P	R	O	Ç	A	Y

▶ Mini-test

Well done – you have completed Unit 2. Now you will be able to order drinks in a café or bar. Let's see what you can remember. Give yourself a point for each of the following questions that you answer correctly in Turkish.

1 How do you call the waiter to your table?
2 How do you ask for a Turkish coffee with, or without, sugar?
3 Ask for a white instant coffee.
4 How do you order a glass of tea?
5 Ask for a glass of red wine and a glass of white wine.
6 How do you ask the waiter for some snacks?
7 Say 'enjoy your drink / meal'.
8 Ask for the bill.
9 Tell the waiter / waitress to keep the change.
10 How do you say 50, 70, 90 and 100?

Points:_____/10

03

accommodation

In this unit you will learn
- how to enquire about accommodation
- how to choose somewhere to stay
- how to ask about the facilities
- how to check in
- how to fill in forms
- telephone numbers
- numbers – hundreds and thousands
- pronunciation: **f, g, ğ**

▶ Dialogue 1 Which hotel?

Ben and Laura are visiting Istanbul. They are brother and sister and are both in their early thirties. They are at the tourist office in **Sultan Ahmet Square** looking for accommodation. If you have the recording, listen to it a couple of times, read it through, then see if you can answer the questions.

Ben   Merhaba.
Memur   Merhaba, efendim.
Ben   Kalacak yerler listesi var mı, lütfen?
Memur   Otel, pansiyon veya kamp?
Ben   Otel, lütfen.
Memur   Buyrun.
Ben   Hangi otel yakın?
Memur   'Yeşil Ev' çok yakın.
Ben   Nasıl yazılır, lütfen?
Memur   Y – e – ş – i – l E – v.
Ben   Teşekkürler.
Memur   İşte harita, bu 'Danışma' ve bu da 'Yeşil Ev'.
Ben   Ah! Harika, çok teşekkürler.

They walk towards the hotel. Ben wonders which building the hotel is.

Ben   Hangi bina acaba?
Laura   Şu bina galiba.

Ben reads the sign above the hotel.

Ben   Evet, o bina.

Questions

1 Otel listesi var mı?
2 Hangi otel yakın?
3 Yeşil Ev nasıl yazılır?
4 Yeşil Ev ne?

kalacak yer listesi	*lists of accommodation*
otel	*hotel*
pansiyon	*guest house*
veya	*or*
kamp	*campsite*
hangi?	*which?*
yakın	*near*
Yeşil Ev	*Green House*
nasıl yazılır?	*how do you spell it?*

çok	*very*
işte	*here*
harita	*map*
bu	*this*
danışma	*information*
ve	*and*
harika	*wonderful*
bina	*building*
acaba	*I wonder*
şu	*that*
galiba	*I think*
o	*that* (referring to something relatively far away)

▶ Dialogue 2 Do you have a vacant room?

Listen to the dialogue a couple of times, then read it through.

Ben and Laura enter the hotel and are at the reception desk.

Ben	İyi akşamlar.
Receptionist	İyi akşamlar, efendim.
Ben	Boş oda var mı?
Receptionist	Kaç kişi?

Ben	Ben ve kardeşim, tek kişilik, iki ayrı oda.
Receptionist	Maalesef, tek kişilik iki oda yok. Ama iki tek yataklı büyük bir oda var.

Ben and Laura are undecided, so the receptionist shows them the room.

Receptionist	Balkonlu ve deniz manzaralı.
Laura	Banyo ve sıcak su var mı?
Receptionist	Evet. Hem küvet hem duş var. Her zaman sıcak su var.
Ben	(*to Laura*) Bu oda güzel, değil mi?
Laura	Evel. Ne kadar?
Receptionist	120 dolar.
Laura	Kahvaltı dahil mi?
Receptionist	Evet, kahvaltı dahil.
Laura	Evet. Tamam.

They go back down to reception.

Receptionist	Kaç gece?
Ben	Üç gece.
Receptionist	Pasaportlar, lütfen?
Ben	Tabii, işte pasaportlar.

They put the passports on the counter.

Receptionist	Teşekkürler.

The receptionist starts filling in the hotel forms. While doing so she repeats some of the sections of the form out loud.

Receptionist	Doğum yeri ... doğum tarihi ... milliyet ... pasaport numarası ... (*Turning to Ben and Laura*) Oda, 24 numara.

She hands them the key for room number 24.

Receptionist	Buyrun, anahtar.
Laura	Valizler?
Receptionist	Mehmet! (*She calls Mehmet, the porter, to carry their suitcases.*)

Questions

1 Boş oda var mı?
2 Oda nasıl?
3 Kaç gece?
4 Kahvaltı dahil mi?

boş	*vacant*
oda	*room*
kaç kişi?	*how many people?*
kardeşim	*my sister / my brother*
tek kişilik	*a single*

ayrı	separate
maalesef	unfortunately (a polite remark)
ama	but
tek yataklı	a single bed
büyük	big
balkonlu	with a balcony
deniz	sea
manzaralı	with a view
banyo	bathroom
sıcak	hot
hem ... hem	both ... and
küvet	bath
duş	shower
her zaman	always
ne kadar?	how much?
kahvaltı	breakfast
dahil/ dahil mi?	included / is it included?
tamam	OK
pasaport	passport
işte	here it is
doğum yeri	place of birth
doğum tarihi	date of birth
milliyet	nationality
pasaport numarası	passport number
numara	number
anahtar	key
valiz	suitcase

Language points

▶ The Turkish alphabet: revision

When booking accommodation or tickets you may be asked to spell your name or you may want to know how the name of a hotel is spelt. If someone wants to know the spelling of a word they simply say, 'nasıl yazılır?' Remember that an English speaker can produce the sounds of all the letters in the **Türkçe alfabe** – it just takes practice. Keep practising until you feel confident with the sounds of all the letters.

Here are the letters of the **Turkish alphabet**. Each letter is followed by a Turkish name so that you can practise the sound in context.

A	B	C	Ç	D	E
a	be	ce	çe	de	e
Asu	Banu	Cengiz	Çetin	Deniz	Emel

F	G	Ğ[1]	H	I	İ
fe	ge		he	ı	i
Fazilet	Gül		Hatice	Işık	İnci

J	K	L	M	N	O
je	ka	le	me	ne	o
Jale	Kaya	Lale	Meral	Nesrin	Osman

Ö	P	R	S	Ş	T
ö	pe	re	se	şe	te
Ömer	Perihan	Recep	Sezgin	Şule	Timur

U	Ü	V	Y	Z
u	ü	ve	ye	ze
Ufuk	Ülkü	Veysel	Yeşim	Zerrin

[1] Ğ has no distinct pronunciation. It makes the previous vowel longer. One example would be sağ, which is pronounced as 'saa'. There is no Turkish word which starts with ğ.

Kaç? *How many? How much?*

Kaç is a useful little word which means *how many* or *how much?*

Kaç lira? *How many lira?* Kaç kişi? *How many people?*
Kaç gece? *How many nights?* Kaç gün? *How many days?*

▶ Dialogue 3 There are lots of good campsites

Banu and Şafak are at a tourist information office in İzmir enquiring about accommodation. Listen to the dialogue a couple of times, read it through then answer the questions.

Şafak   Merhaba.
Clerk   İyi günler.
Şafak   Kalacak otel ve kamp listesi var mı?
Clerk   Var. Bu otel listesi.
They both look at the list.
Banu   Oteller biraz pahalı.
Clerk   Çok güzel kamplar var ve çok ucuz. Buyrun işte bu liste adresler ve telefon numaraları.

Banu asks politely if there is a telephone at the office.

Banu Telefon var mı, acaba?
Clerk Evet. İşte orada. (*The clerk points out the telephone.*)
Şafak Kart var mı?[2]
Clerk Evet. 10 milyon lira.[3]
Şafak Bir kart, lütfen.

The clerk gives him the telephone card. He dials the number.

Kamp Alo ... 752 52 06 Truva Kamping. Buyrun.
Şafak Alo. Ben Şafak Gezer. İki kişilik çadır var mı?
Kamp Evet, var. Kaç günlük?
Şafak Beş gün.
Kamp Tamam.
Şafak Kampta neler var? Elektrik var mı?
Kamp Tabii. Devamlı elektrik, su ve sıcak su var. Restoran, yüzme-havuzu, plaj, duşlar, çocuk oyun parkı, ilk yardım ve genel telefon da var.
Şafak Tamam. Yarın sabah görüşürüz.
Kamp Tamam. Adınız, lütfen?
Şafak Adım Şafak, soyadım Gezer.
Kamp Efendim? Nasıl yazılır?
Şafak Ş – a – f – a – k G – e – z – e – r.

[2]You need a telephone card to use a public telephone in Turkey.
[3]You will often see 'TL'. It stands for 'Turkish lira'.

Questions

1 Telefon var mı?
2 Kampta su var mı?
3 Kampta neler var?

biraz	*a little*
pahalı	*expensive*
ucuz	*cheap*
liste	*list*
adres	*address*
telefon numaraları	*telephone numbers*
orada	*there*
alo	*hello (on the phone)*
çadır	*tent*
kaç günlük?	*how many days?*
kampta	*at the campsite*
elektrik	*electricity*
devamlı	*continuous*
yüzme-havuzu	*swimming pool*
ilk yardım	*first aid post*

plaj	*beach*
çocuk	*child*
oyun parkı	*play area*
genel telefon	*a public phone*
da	*also*
yarın	*tomorrow*
sabah	*morning*
görüşürüz	*see you*
adınız	*your name*
adım	*my name (first name)*
soyadım	*my surname*
efendim?	*pardon?*
tekrar	*again*

Language points

Telephone numbers

Turkish telephone numbers usually have seven digits, plus an area code where appropriate. When giving a telephone number, it is usual to break it down into three digits, two digits and two digits. You learnt how to say two-digit numbers in Unit 2, and in this unit you will learn how to say three-digit numbers. Listen again to the campsite manager answering Şafak's telephone call and notice how she breaks down the number.

▶ More numbers – hundreds and thousands

First read and listen to these numbers, then pause the recording and repeat each number after the speaker. Do this as many times as you need to, until you feel comfortable with all of the numbers. When you feel confident test yourself. Try saying the numbers from 100 to 9,000, then try saying them from 9,000 down to 100.

100	yüz	1,000	bin
200	ikiyüz	2,000	ikibin
300	üçyüz	3,000	üçbin
400	dörtyüz	4,000	dörtbin
500	beşyüz	5,000	beşbin
600	altıyüz	6,000	altıbin
700	yediyüz	7,000	yedibin
800	sekizyüz	8,000	sekizbin
900	dokuzyüz	9,000	dokuzbin

▶ Dialogue 4 This is your tent

Next day Banu and Şafak arrive at the campsite and the manageress Ayşegül meets them. Listen to the dialogue a couple of times, read it through, answer the questions and check the answers at the back of the book.

Ayşegül	Ben Ayşegül. Hoş geldiniz.
Banu	Ben Banu. (*Points at Şafak.*) O Şafak. (*They shake hands.*)
Banu and Şafak	Hoş bulduk.
Ayşegül	Nasılsınız?
Banu	Biz iyiyiz, teşekkürler. Siz nasılsınız?

Ayşegül smiles.

Ayşegül	Çok meşgulüz.

Ayşegül shows them their tent and the facilities of the campsite.

Ayşegül	Bu sizin çadır, burası araba parkı, o telefon, şurası yüzme-havuzu, ve şu restoran, bunlar tuvaletler, şunlar duşlar, bu bungalov ilk yardım.

They hear a dog barking.

Ayşegül	O da bizim köpek, 'Karabaş'*.

They all laugh.

hav-hav

*Karabaş is a very common name for a dog in Turkish and literally means 'blackhead'.

Questions

1 Yüzme havuzu var mı?
2 Köpek var mı?
3 Kim meşgul?

hoş geldiniz	*welcome*
hoş bulduk	*the set reply to* **hoş geldiniz**
iyiyiz	*we are well*
meşgulüz	*we are busy*
sizin	*your*
burası	*here, this place*
şurası	*there, that place*
bunlar	*these are*
köpek	*dog*

Language points

Personal pronouns

A pronoun is a word that is used instead of a noun:

Ben	*I*	Biz	*we*
Sen	*you*	Siz	*you*
O	*he, she, it*	Onlar	*they*

We learnt about **sen** and **siz** in Unit 1 and now you have met some of the other personal pronouns (**ben, biz, o**). In the dialogue, Banu introduces herself, '**Ben Banu**' *I am Banu*; Banu and Şafak say '**biz iyiyiz**' *we are fine* and Ayşegül introduces the dog '**o da bizim köpek Karabaş**'. You probably noticed that Turkish is simpler than English – no words for *am, are* or *is* are needed!

bu, şu, o *this, that*

Where English has two words for *this* and *that*, Turkish has three. **Bu** means *this (is)* as in **Bu sizin çadır** *this is your tent*, when it is very near. **Şu** means *that (is)*, when you are referring to something fairly near. **O** means *that (is)*, when you are referring to something further away. So when Ayşegül says, '**Şu bungalov, o telefon**' she is indicating that the bungalow is a little way off and the telephone is further away.

Again, Turkish uses fewer words than English as no words are used for *is* or *are*, e.g. **Bu çadır** *this is the tent*. However, you do need to put a plural ending on **bu, şu** or **o** if you are referring to plural nouns. As an example, Ayşegül says '**bunlar tuvaletlar**' *these are the toilets*.

Singular	Plural
bu	bunlar
şu	şunlar
o	onlar

burası, şurası, orası *this, that place*

Three very useful words derived from **bu, şu, o** are **burası, şurası, orası** meaning *this place*, *that place* and *the place over there*. Listen to the recording again. You will hear Ayşegül say '**Burası araba parkı**', *this (place) is the car park*.

Bu şişe su şişesi, şu şişe süt şişesi

▶ Tongue twister

Try this Turkish tongue twister:

Şu şişe su şişesi, şu şişe süt şişcsi.

i Turkey has many organized campsites for tents and caravans, and camping offers a great way to get off the beaten track and see village and country life. In pitching your tent you'd be following a long cultural tradition in Turkey – that of the nomad! Some of the medieval campsites used by ancient travellers along the historic Silk Route are being restored to their former glory – but today's travellers will find plenty of modern campsites, with good facilities, often in beautiful National Parks.

Practice

▶ 1 Read these telephone numbers out loud, then compare your version with the recording. Write down the numbers in words.

Example İncekum   345 14 48   Üçyüzkırkbeş ondört kırksekiz

a	Gökova	246 50 35	....
b	Çamlıköy	262 01 37	....
c	Yat	614 13 33	....
d	V – Camp	717 22 24	....
e	Pamukcak	896 36 36	....
f	Altınkum camp	311 48 57	....

2 Write the numbers below in figures.

a beşyüzotuzbir b dörtyüzkırkdört c altıbinyediyüzellibeş
d binbir   e üçbinotuzüç   f dokuzyüzonaltı
g yedibinsekizyüzondört   h dörtbin

3 Match the Turkish words on the left with the pictures on the
right. The first one has been done for you.

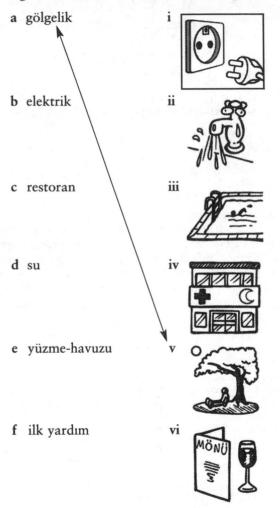

a gölgelik   i

b elektrik   ii

c restoran   iii

d su   iv

e yüzme-havuzu   v

f ilk yardım   vi

4 Match the Turkish and the English words. The first one has been done for you.

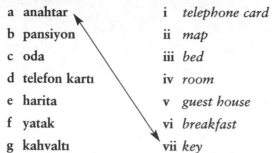

a **anahtar**   i *telephone card*

b **pansiyon**   ii *map*

c **oda**   iii *bed*

d **telefon kartı**   iv *room*

e **harita**   v *guest house*

f **yatak**   vi *breakfast*

g **kahvaltı**   vii *key*

▶ **5 Pronunciation: f, g, ğ.** First, listen to the recording, then listen while looking at the following sounds and finally listen and repeat.

f	g	ğ
af	ege	sağ
fa	gel	dağ
fil	lig	ağa
üf	göz	ağrı
uf	gül	

6 Write the Turkish for the following.

a I am   e it is

b you are   f we are

c he is   g you are

d she is   h they are

7 Wordsearch. Find ten words connected with hotels. The first has been done for you.

A	R	O	O	T	E	L	F	G	T
D	R	A	T	Y	O	F	C	Ç	E
U	P	S	T	R	S	A	E	A	P
S	Z	A	N	A	H	T	A	R	E
M	A	N	Z	A	R	A	L	I	K
P	Y	A	T	A	K	F	B	R	Ü
B	A	L	K	O	N	L	U	O	V
K	O	S	Y	I	D	S	R	D	E
K	A	H	V	A	L	T	I	A	T
E	P	A	N	S	İ	Y	O	N	Z

▶ Mini-test

Congratulations; you have now completed Unit 3. Now you will be able to choose your accommodation, make enquiries about it, book it and give your telephone number. Give yourself a point for each of the following questions that you answer correctly in Turkish.

1 Ask for a room with a shower.
2 Ask whether the hotel has a vacant room.
3 Ask if breakfast is included.
4 Ask someone how you spell a word.
5 How do you say *this* and *that*?
6 How do you say *I, you, he, she, it, we, you* (plural) and *they* in Turkish?

Points:_____/6

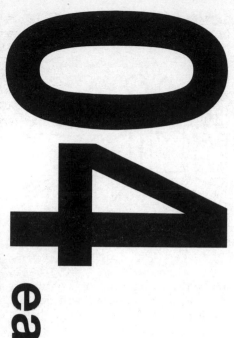

In this unit you will learn
- how to order meals
- how to enquire what dishes there are and what's in them
- how to pay the bill
- pronunciation: h, ı, i

▶ Dialogue 1 Ordering breakfast

Ben and Laura decide to have a typical Turkish breakfast in the hotel garden.

If you have the recording, listen to the dialogue a couple of times and see if you can answer the following questions with **doğru** *true* or **yanlış** *false* before reading the dialogue. This will help you to practise understanding spoken Turkish.

True or false?

1 Çay var.
2 Çay çok lezzetli.

Listen to the dialogue again, then read it through, and see if you can answer the questions at the end.

Laura   Bahçede kahvaltı çok hoş.
Ben   Evet. Hava ne güzel!
Waiter   Günaydın, efendim.
Ben   Günaydın. Bizim için Türk kahvaltısı, lütfen.
Waiter   Tabii, efendim.
Laura   Kahvaltıda neler var?
The waiter brings the breakfast on a trolley.
Waiter   Tereyağı, bal, marmelat, reçel, peynir, zeytin, sosis.
Ben   Sucuk yok mu?
Waiter   Var, efendim. Salam, domates, salatalık, biber. Ve taze ekmek de var tabii.
Ben   Çay var mı?
Waiter   Tabii.
He pours their tea into tulip-shaped glasses.
Laura   Teşekkürler.
Laura has a sip of the tea.

Laura	Çay çok lezzetli.
Waiter	Afiyet olsun, efendim.

The waiter puts the breakfast on the table.

Waiter	Yumurta?
Laura	Hayır, teşekkürler.
Ben	Evet, bana rafadan lütfen.
Waiter	Tabii, efendim.
Ben	Sucuk da çok lezzetli.
Laura	Tuz yok mu?
Ben	İşte masada canım.

The waiter puts the toast on the table.

Waiter	Buyrun kızarmış ekmekler de burada. Afiyet olsun. Başka?
Laura	Yok. Teşekkürler.

Questions

3 Hava nasıl?
4 Kahvaltıda neler var?
5 Kahvaltıda bal ve reçel var mı?
6 Tuz nerede?

bizim için	*for us*
Türk kahvaltısı	*Turkish breakfast*
kahvaltıda	*at breakfast*
neler?	*What is there?*
tereyağı	*butter*
bal	*honey*
marmelat	*marmalade*
reçel	*jam*
peynir	*cheese*
zeytin	*olives*
sosis	*sausage*
sucuk	*spicy Turkish sausage*
yok mu?	*isn't there any?*
salam	*salami*
domates	*tomatoes*
salatalık	*cucumber*
biber	*pepper*
taze	*fresh*
ekmek	*bread*
yumurta	*egg*
bana	*for me*
rafadan	*soft-boiled egg*
da	*also, too*

lezzetli	*tasty*
tuz	*salt*
masada	*on the table*
kızarmış	*toasted*
burada	*here*
başka?	*anything else?*
yok	*no, not, there isn't, etc.*

i A typical Turkish **kahvaltı** *breakfast* consists of **çay** *tea*, with **ekmek** *bread* or **kızarmış ekmek** *toast* (literally *reddened bread*), **tereyağı** *butter*, **bal** *honey* or **reçel** *jam*. **Gül reçeli** *rose petal jam*, **incir reçeli** *fig jam* and **vişne reçeli** *sour cherry jam* are worth trying. **Peynir** *cheese* and **zeytin** *olives* are usually served at breakfast, too. You can also ask for **yumurta** *eggs*, either **rafadan** *soft boiled*, **katı** *hard boiled* or **yağda** *fried*.

Language points

-de, -da *at, on, in*

In Turkish to say *at*, *on*, or *in* you put the ending **-de**, **-da** on the noun instead of using a separate word. Here are some examples:

Kahvaltı masada.	*Breakfast is on the table.*
Kahvaltıda neler var?	*What is there for breakfast.*
Restoranda.	*At the restaurant.*
Otelde.	*At the hotel.*

To decide whether to use **-de** or **-da** on the end of a word, you simply choose the one which harmonizes best with the *last vowel* in that word:

- **da** harmonizes best with (**a, ı, o, u**)
- **de** harmonizes best with (**e, i, ö, ü**).

It helps if you can remember these groups but don't worry too much about it. The more you are exposed to the language (particularly the more you hear it), the easier it will become to know which ending to use. This is the same principle as with the **-ler**, **-lar** endings which we looked at in Unit 2 (the first rule of vowel harmony).

▶ Dialogue 2 At a fish restaurant

Ahmet and Yeşim decide to go to a **balık restoranı** *fish restaurant* with their friends Vanessa and Asuman. Yeşim makes the reservation for four people and they meet at the restaurant at 8 p.m. As they are going to have a few drinks, Ahmet does not take his car. If you have the recording, listen to it a couple of times, then answer the following questions with **doğru** *true* or **yanlış** *false*.

True or false?

1 Çankaya var.
2 Su var.

Listen to the dialogue again, then read it through and see if you can answer the questions at the end.

Ahmet	Garson, lütfen.
Waiter	Buyrun, efendim.
Ahmet	Şarap ne var?
Waiter	Çankaya ve Kutman çok güzel.
Yeşim	Çankaya, lütfen.
Asuman	Bana da beyaz Çankaya, lütfen.
Ahmet	Ya sen, Vanessa?
Vanessa	Vişne suyu, lütfen.

Ahmet orders the drinks first.

Ahmet	Bir büyük, beyaz Çankaya. Bir küçük rakı, ve bir de vişne suyu.
Waiter	Hemen, efendim.
Ahmet	Bir şişe de su tabii.

The waiter goes to fetch the drinks. They look at the **balık mönü** *(fish menu) and are ready to order when the waiter returns.*

Ahmet	Bana kalkan tava ve karışık salata, lütfen.
Asuman	Bana levrek buğulama ve yeşil salata, lütfen.
Vanessa	Bana da barbunya tava ve dilimlenmiş domates, lütfen.
Yeşim	Lüfer ızgara ve roka, lütfen.
Waiter	Tabii, efendim.

They all enjoy their meal. At the end of the meal they have **karışık meyve** *(mixed fruit) followed by* **Türk kahvesi** *(Turkish coffee).*

Ahmet	Garson, hesap, lütfen.
Waiter	Buyrun, hesap.

Ahmet pays the bill and leaves a tip.

Ahmet	Teşekkürler. Üstü kalsın.

The waiter is pleased with the tip.

Waiter	Sağ olun, efendim.

Ahmet	Taksi nerede?
Waiter	Burada, sağda, efendim.

Questions

3 Çankaya şarap mı?
4 Vanessa için vişne suyu mu?
5 Yeşim Hanım için lüfer tava mı?
6 Yeşil salata Ahmet Bey için mi?

ya sen?	and you?
hemen	straight away
balık	fish
kalkan	turbot
karışık salata	mixed salad
levrek	bass
buğulama	steamed
barbunya	red mullet
tava	fried
dilimlenmiş	sliced
domates	tomatoes
lüfer	blue fish
ızgara	grilled
roka	rocket leaves
Üstü kalsın.	Keep the change.
taksi	taxi
nerede	where?
burada	here
sağda	on the right

i In the evenings you will find restaurants serving **sıcak ve soğuk meze** (*hot and cold hors d'oeuvres*). Restaurants often serve grilled meat or fish as a main course after the **meze**. If you want to ensure being served good, fresh fish it is best to go to a **balık lokantası** (*fish restaurant*). You can often choose the fish you want before it is cooked. Try ordering your fish in Turkish – Turks will love it if you make an effort to speak some Turkish. If in return they want to practise their English, don't give up with your Turkish!

Customer	Bu ne?	*What's this?*
Waiter	Bu mu?	*This one?*
Customer	Evet.	*Yes.*
Waiter	Lüfer	*Blue fish.*
Customer	O büyük lüfer, lütfen.	*That big blue fish, please.*

You will often be asked how you want the fish cooked, and you can generally choose from **ızgara** *grilled*, **tava** *fried*, **buğulama** *steamed* or **kiremitte** baked on a tile in the oven.

Rakı *aniseed-flavoured spirit* is the normal drink with fish. Most Turks drink **rakı** with water.

▶ Dialogue 3 At a *köfte* restaurant

Following their visit to the Basilica cistern (a Byzantine underground reservoir) Ben and Laura are now feeling hungry. They can't decide whether to have lunch at a **köfte** restaurant (which specializes in various types of meatball) or **muhallebici** (shops which sell puddings and savoury pastries).

If you have the recording, listen to it a couple of times, then answer the questions below with **doğru** *true*, or **yanlış** *false*.

True or false?

1 The beer is cold.
2 The view is beautiful.

Ben	Muhallebici mi, köfteci mi?
Laura	Öğlen köfteci, akşam muhallebici.
Ben	Tamam. Hadi.

They go to the famous Sultan Ahmet Köftecisi, which overlooks the Blue Mosque. They ask if the restaurant has **cız bız köfte** *grilled meatballs.*

Ben	Cız bız köfte var mı?
Waiter	Var, efendim. Kaç porsiyon?
Laura	İki porsiyon, pilavlı.
Waiter	Tabii, efendim.
Laura	(*to Ben*) Bira mı, ayran mı?
Ben	Bira soğuk mu?
Waiter	Evet, çok soğuk.
Ben	Benim için, bir soğuk bira.
Laura	Bana da bir soğuk ayran, lütfen.
Waiter	Başka?

They look at the menu.

Ben	Piyaz var mı?
Waiter	Var, efendim.
Ben	Bana bir piyaz.
Laura	Bana da karışık salata.

The waiter brings their order to the table.

Waiter	Afiyet olsun.
Ben and Laura	Teşekkür! Teşekkürler!

| Laura | Köfte çok lezzetli, değil mi? |
| Ben | Evet, çok. |

Listen to the dialogue again, then read through it and see if you can answer the following questions:

Questions

3 Kaç porsiyon köfte?
4 Piyaz ne?
5 Köfte güzel mi?

öğlen	noon
hadi	come on
cız bız	sizzling / fried
porsiyon	portion
pilavlı	with cooked rice
benim için	for me
bana da	for me too
başka	anything else
piyaz	white bean salad

Language points

Making questions with mı (mi, mu, mü)

In general **mı, mi, mu, mü** appear after nouns (naming words), verbs (doing words) and adjectives (describing words) to make a question. Simply choose the one which rhymes best with the *last vowel* in the word before:

Balık mı?	(Is it) fish?
Şeftali mi?	(Is it) peach?
Karpuz mu?	(Is it) watermelon?
Üzüm mü?	(Are they) grapes?

The examples above are quite straightforward as the two vowels which need to rhyme are exactly the same. Sometimes, however, the last vowel of the preceding word may be **a, e, o** or **ö**. In such cases you use the form which sounds the closest. For example:

Çay mı?	Tea?
Ekmek mi?	Bread?
Tost mu?	Toasted sandwich?
Likör mü?	Liqueur?

- **mı** comes after ı, a
- **mi** comes after i, e
- **mu** comes after u, o
- **mü** comes after ü, ö

This follows the second rule of vowel harmony. The word **mi** is an i-type ending word.

Do not try to learn the rules of vowel harmony by heart. Whenever you hear or read Turkish, you will come across them and you will come to know which endings to use instinctively. Meanwhile, as a beginner and a foreign language learner there is little to worry about, as even if you do not harmonize your vowels correctly, it will not affect the actual meaning of what you say and people will still understand you! Everyone makes mistakes.

ℹ️ The Turks are very creative people when it comes to food. **Sebze** *vegetables*, **et** *meat*, **pilav** (cooked rice, vermicelli or cracked wheat, plain or with small pieces of vegetables or meat) and **börek** *pastry* are the main features of Turkish cuisine. Bread is served with almost everything, as is a glass of water.

Every visitor should try **börek**. These are delicious savouries made out of thin layers of pastry with minced meat, vegetable, cheese, or onion fillings. They are cooked in the oven or fried individually. You can find them at a **börekçi** *pastry shop*, **pastane** *cake shop* or **fırın** *bakery*.

Other foods to look out for include **pide**. This is a Turkish pizza made of flat baked bread. You can have **kıymalı pide** *with minced meat*, **peynirli pide** *with cheese*, **yumurtalı pide** *with egg*. You can have a takeaway or sit and eat it in a **pideci** *a Turkish pizza restaurant*. You will also find **lahmacun** served in **pideci**. These are thin savoury pancakes baked in the oven, covered with minced meat, tomatoes and chopped onion. They are accompanied by fresh parsley and lemon. Vegetable dishes are plentiful, but strict vegetarians should ask for them to be **zeytinyağlı** *cooked with olive oil* rather than meat stock. These dishes are served cold. If you want to ask what vegetarian options are available you can say, **'Etsiz yemek ne var?'** *'What vegetarian dishes do you have?'*

In Turkish, two words are used for restaurant – **restoran** and **lokanta**. **Restoran** is more frequently used in tourist areas and big cities, and the restaurants are usually proud to display their star ratings at the entrance and on the menu: **lüks** *luxury*, **1nci sınıf** *first class*, **2nci sınıf** *second class*. **Lokanta** is more often used for local or rural restaurants and cafés.

In a restaurant the simplest way of attracting the waiter's attention is to call **'Garson'** *'Waiter'*, and to order something, you can just name it. To be more polite, you can add **lütfen** *please*. You normally pay in cafés and restaurants when you're ready to leave. Restaurant prices include **KDV** *VAT*. A 10% **bahşiş** *tip* is usual and much appreciated.

Practice

1 Memory game. Look at the picture of the breakfast on the table at the beginning of the unit for three minutes then turn back to this page and see how much you can remember. Write down in Turkish what was on the table. When you can't remember any more items, have another look at the picture for a further two minutes and then write down anything you missed.

2 Make questions using (-mı, -mi, -mu or -mü). Use the endings (-mı, -mi, -mu, -mü) to complete the following questions. You may need to use each ending more than once. The first one has been done for you.

   a Kahvaltı güzel __mi__ ?
   b Karışık meyve _____ ?
   c Balık lezetli _____?
   d Pide ucuz_____?
   e O biber mi, tuz _____?
   f Otel lüks _____?

3 Reorder the following sentences below to form a meaningful dialogue.

   a Garson.
   b Karışık meyve var mı?
   c Bir karışık meyve, lütfen.
   d Buyrun?
   e Var.
   f Tabii efendim.

4 Look at the pictures and complete the accompanying sentences.

   a Bir bardak _____, lütfen.

b İki porsiyon _____, lütfen.

c Karışık _____, lütfen.

d Daha _____, lütfen.

5 Answer these questions with **evet** *yes* or **hayır** *no*. The first one has been done for you.

a Yeşil Ev İstanbul'da mı? ☺ Evet, İstanbul'da.
b Rakı soğuk mu? ☺
c Döner et mi? ☺
d Karpuz ucuz mu? ☺
e Şeftali sebze mi? ☹
f Salata lezzetli mi? ☺
g Lokum alkollü mü? ☹
h Baklava tatlı mı? ☺
i Zeytin siyah mı? ☹
j Simit taze mi? ☺

6 Match the Turkish words with their corresponding picture.
The first one has been done for you.

a balık

b üzüm

c salam

d domates

e karpuz

f ekmek

i

ii

iii

iv

v

vi

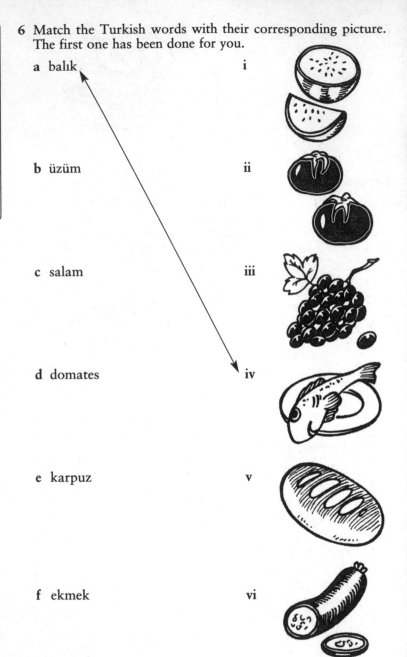

▶ **7 Pronunciation: h, ı, i.** First, listen without looking, then listen while looking. Finally listen and repeat.

h	ı	i
ah	ısı	bir
hey	sık	iki
daha	ılık	pis
höt	kış	pil

▶ Mini-test

Well done; you have completed Unit 4. Now you will be able to order your meals, ask what dishes there are and pay the bill. Give yourself a point for each if you can say these things in Turkish without looking at the back.

1 Order a breakfast of coffee, butter, bread, sausages and egg.
2 Order fried fish with a green salad.
3 Order a large white wine.
4 Order two portions of meatballs with cooked rice.
5 Ask if the beer is cold.

Points:_____/5

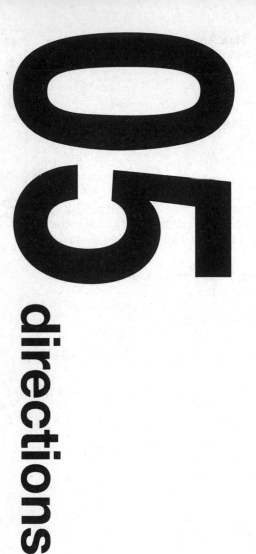

05
directions

In this unit you will learn
- how to ask for, and give, directions
- how to get around a new place
- how to ask what something means
- pronunciation: j, k, l

▶Dialogue 1 At the airport

Dr Bahadır Bey and his wife Ülkü have just landed at Istanbul Airport. They are looking for the bank and they ask someone for directions.

First listen to the dialogue a couple of times and then read through it. See if you can understand the conversation with the aid of the words in the vocabulary box. If you need more help, look at the translation at the back of the book.

Bahadır	Afedersiniz, banka nerede, acaba?
Passer-by	Özür dilerim. Bilmiyorum. Danışmaya sorun. Danışma orada.
Bahadır	Çok teşekkürler.

They ask at the information desk where the bank and the toilets are.

Ülkü	Afedersiniz, banka nerede, acaba?
Clerk	Düz gidin, pasaport kontrolu geçin ve gümrüklerden sonra sağa dönün, tekrar düz gidin, solda.
Ülkü	Aaa, çok teşekkürler. En yakın tuvalet nerede, acaba?
Clerk	Düz gidin, pasaport kontroldan önce, sağda ve solda iki tuvalet var. Pasaport kontroldan sonra iki tuvalet daha var.
Bahadır	Çok teşekkürler.
Clerk	Bir şey değil.
Bahadır	Taksiler nerede acaba?
Clerk	Kapıdan çıkın, yolu geçin, orada.

Bahadır and Ülkü get into a taxi.

Driver	Nereye, efendim?
Bahadır	Sultan Ahmet'e, lütfen. Sultan Ahmet uzak mı?
Driver	Biraz – 20 kilometre, 40 dakika falan.

Atatürk Havalimanı

A	Geliş İskelesi	Arrivals Bridge
B	Vize Ofisi	Visa Office
C	Bagaj Alım Bantı	Incoming Baggage Band
D	Otel Reservasyon	Hotel Reservation
E	Banka	Bank
F	Alış Veriş Merkezi	Shopping Centre
G	Yemek Alanları	Food Courts
H	Tuvaletler	Toilets
I	Kayıp Bagaj	Lost Luggage
J	Emanet	Luggage Custody
K	Oto Kiralama	Rent-A-Car
L	CIP Salonları	VIP Lounges
M	Transit Yolcu Bankosu	Transit Passenger Lounge
N	Merdivenler	Escalators

Questions

Read the dialogue above and look at the plan of Istanbul Airport carefully. Were Bahadır and Ülkü given the correct directions for these places?

1 Banka.
2 Tuvaletler.
3 Taksiler.

afedersiniz*	*excuse me*
banka	*bank*
özür dilerim	*I'm sorry*
bilmiyorum	*I don't know*
düz	*straight*
gidin	*go (polite instruction)*
pasaport kontrol	*passport control*
geçmek	*to cross*
gümrük	*customs*
-den / -dan sonra	*after ...*
-den / -dan önce	*before ...*
sağ	*right*
dönmek	*to turn / return*
sol	*left*
en	*most*

en yakın	*nearest*
tuvalet	*toilet*
daha	*more*
taksi	*taxi*
çık<u>mak</u>	<u>*to*</u> *come out*
yol	*road*
uzak	*far*
biraz	*a little*
dakika	*minute*
falan	*roughly / or so*

*In spoken Turkish, **afedersiniz** has one 'f'; in written Turkish it appears as **affedersiniz**.

i General information about Turkey and basic maps are available from the **turizm bürosu** *Turkish tourist offices*, abroad and in Turkey. When you need to ask something, the easiest way to attract attention is to say, '**Afedersiniz**' *'excuse me'* followed by your question. To ask where something is, say the word for what you're looking for, followed by **nerede** *where?*, e.g. **Giriş nerede?** *Where is the entrance?*, **Gişe nerede?** *Where is the ticket office?* When you're being given directions, listen out for the important bits such as whether to turn right or left, and try to repeat each bit to make sure you've understood it correctly. You can always ask the person to say it again more slowly: **bir daha lütfen** *once more, please*; **daha yavaş** *more slowly*. If you are looking for a **tuvalet** *toilet* they are sometimes labelled **baylar** *gents*, **bayanlar** *ladies* or **erkek** *men* and **kadın** *women*. They may also be marked with the sign **00**.

Language points

Verbs

Verbs are action words such as *go*, *do*, *walk*, and in Turkish they generally come at the end of sentences. Verbs change according to who does the action and / or when it happens. When you look up a verb in an English dictionary you see the main part or the stem of the verb with 'to' in front of it, e.g. to mean, to ask. The dictionary form of Turkish verbs is the stem plus the ending -**mek** or -**mak**. Dictionary forms are sometimes called the infinitive. Sometimes the dictionary form is used as it stands, and sometimes you use it to make the correct form of the verb.

You will notice that some verbs have -**mek** endings while some have -**mak** endings. This is our old friend vowel harmony again! The ending is the one which rhymes best with the *last* vowel in that word, so it depends on the last vowel in the stem of the verb:

- -**mak** harmonizes best with **a, ı, o, u**
- -**mek** harmonizes best with **e, i, ö, ü.**

Commands and instructions

In Turkish, you give informal commands such as **Git!** *Go!* by using the verb stem. You make the stem by taking the dictionary form of the verb and removing -**mek** or -**mak**. For example, the verb stem of **sormak** *to ask* is **sor** *ask*! and the verb stem of **dönmek** *to turn* is **dön** *turn*!

Here are some infinitives and their corresponding informal commands:

sormak	*to ask*	**Sor!**	*Ask!*
gitmek	*to go*	**Git!**	*Go!*
geçmek	*to cross*	**Geç!**	*Cross!*
dönmek	*to turn*	**Dön!**	*Turn!*
çıkmak	*to come out / go up*	**Çık!**	*Come out!*
girmek	*to enter*	**Gir!**	*Enter!*
bırakmak	*to leave*	**Bırak!**	*Leave!*

Formal or informal?

As you know, there are two ways of saying *you* (**sen** and **siz**) in Turkish, one formal and the other informal. You will, therefore, need to learn two ways of telling people what to do – one polite or formal, one friendly or informal. Here is the friendly or informal way:

Sor!	*Ask!*
Geç!	*Cross!*
Dön!	*Turn!*
Çık!	*Come out!*

To make the command politer use the **siz** form. Take the verb stem (which is also the friendly form of command) and add -**in**, -**ın**, -**un** or -**ün**.

On warning signs and official notices you will see a third very formal form of command, using the following endings -ınız, -iniz, -unuz, -ünüz. You will probably never need to use this form yourself, but you do need to recognize it.

Vowel harmony yet again determines which ending to use. Choose the one which rhymes best with the last vowel in that word, following the rules of i-type vowel harmony:

- -ın and -ınız harmonizes with / comes after a, ı
- -un and -unuz harmonizes with / comes after u, o
- -in and -iniz harmonizes with / comes after i, e
- -ün and -ünüz harmonizes / comes after ü, ö

Polite commands	Very formal commands
Sorun!	Sorunuz!
Geçin!	Geçiniz!
Dönün!	Dönünüz!
Çıkın!	Çıkınız!

▶ Dialogue 2 In Sultan Ahmet Square

Bahadır and Ülkü are in Sultan Ahmet Square. They ask for directions to some places of interest. If you have the recording, first listen to the dialogue a couple of times, then read the dialogue.

Ülkü   Afedersiniz, Topkapı Müzesi nerede acaba?
Passer-by   Efendim?
Ülkü   Topkapı Müzesi nerede, acaba?
Passer-by   Özür dilerim, bilmiyorum.
They ask someone else.
Ülkü   Afedersiniz, Topkapı nerede, acaba?
Passer-by   Düz gidin, köşede sola dönün tam karşıda.
Ülkü   Müzeler ne zaman açık?
Passer-by   Saat 9'dan 5'e kadar.
Ülkü   Teşekkürler.
Passer-by   Bir şey değil.
They find the Topkapı Palace and go to the ticket office.
Bahadır   İki bilet, lütfen.
Receptionist Buyrun. Çantaları buraya bırakın.
Bahadır   Teşekkürler. Harem nerede?
Receptionist Düz gidin. Orada işaretler var.

Questions

Read the dialogue above and answer these questions in Turkish.

1 Müzeler ne zaman açık?
2 Harem nerede?

müze	*museum*
Topkapı Müzesi	*Topkapı Museum*
özür dilemek	*to apologize*
köşe	*corner*
tam	*right / exactly*
karşı	*opposite*
zaman	*time*
açık	*open*
-den ... -e kadar	*from ... to ...*
bilet	*ticket*
çanta	*bag*
buraya	*here* (shows movement)
bırakmak	*to leave*
Harem	*Harem*
işaret	*sign*

i The Harem was the home of the imperial family. It was like a small villa with up to 500 people living there, including the sultan, his mother, wives, children and up to 300 concubines. The sultan's women were not allowed to enter the outside world and were guarded by a corps of black eunuchs who also acted as go-betweens with the outside world. The Harem was a place of political intrigue. If you want to find out more about life in the Harem, the book *Harem: the world behind the veil*, by Alev Lytle Croutlier is a very interesting read.

Language points

'the'

There is no actual word for *the* in Turkish. But in some cases **-ı**, which has four variations (**-ı, -i, u, ü**), is used as a word ending to give the same meaning. These endings are principally used when the verb has a direct object (see below). The **-i** ending follows **i**-type vowel harmony.

Işıkları geç.	*Pass the lights.*
Müzeyi geç.	*Pass the museum.*
Yolu geç.	*Cross the road.*
Otobüsü sür.	*Drive the bus.*

Direct objects

In Turkish it is important to spot the direct object of a verb. A direct object is something or someone which is having an action carried out on it, as in *Kate sees the sun*. There are direct objects in these commands:

Camiyi geç.	*Pass the mosque.*
Çayı iç.	*Drink the tea.*
Üzümü ye.	*Eat the grapes.*

In these examples the direct objects are the things that are to be passed, drunk and eaten (the mosque, the tea and the grapes).

Saying 'the'

Turkish does not usually distinguish between *a* and *the*. In the case of the direct object of a verb, however, Turkish *does* make a distinction: in this case it needs the equivalent of *the*. For direct objects, the Turkish equivalent of *the* is the ending -i (-ı, -u, -ü) (or -yi (-ı, -u, -ü) if the noun ends in a vowel). As we mentioned in Unit 2, the equivalent of *a* is either **bir** or nothing.

For example:

Çay iç.	*Drink (some) tea.*
Bir çay iç.	*Drink a (one) tea.*
Çayı iç.	*Drink the tea.*

Araba sür.	*Drive a car.*
Bir araba sür.	*Drive a car.*
Arabayı sür.	*Drive the car.*

You use *the* in English to talk about *specific* items. Likewise in Turkish, you use the -i (-ı, -u, -ü) ending if the direct object is a *specific* item.

At this stage, don't worry about getting these endings right. People will understand you. Just try to notice them when you hear or see them. Some commands do not have direct objects:

Git!	Go.
Çık!	*Come out / Get out!*
Dikkat et!	*Watch out! Pay attention! Be careful!*

Word order

Although Turkish word order is relatively free and flexible, it is best to follow the main principle that verbs go at the end of the sentence.

Git.	Go.
Sen git.	*You go.*
Sen müzeye git.	*You go to the museum.* (lit. you museum to go.)

The basic word order is subject (the person or thing performing the action) followed by the object (the person or thing having the action done to it), and the verb (the action word) goes at the end of the sentence. Remember this easily by SOV (Subject – Object – Verb). Word order is described in more detail in Unit 7 and in *Teach Yourself Turkish*.

▶ Dialogue 3 Blue Cruise

Ülkü and Bahadır are at a tourist office in Bodrum, enquiring about cruises along the coast, known as 'Blue Cruises'.

Ülkü Afedersiniz, Bodrum'dan Mavi Yolculuk var mı?
Clerk Var.
Ülkü Nereye var?
Clerk Birincisi, Bodrum'dan Ören'e, Ören'den Körmen'e, Körmen'den tekrar Bodrum'a. İkincisi, Bodrum'dan Karaada'ya, Karaada'dan Cedre'ye, Cedre'den Ballısu'ya, Ballısu'dan Bodrum'a.
Ülkü Aaa! Birinci güzel! Liman nerede?
Clerk Sahilde, merkezde.
Ülkü Teşekkürler.
Clerk Rica ederim.

Questions

Read the dialogue and try to answer the following questions.

1 Bodrum'dan Mavi Yolculuk var mı?
2 Liman nerede?

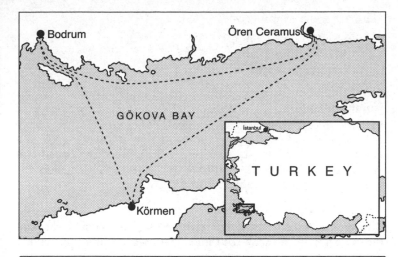

Mavi Yolculuk	*Blue Cruise*
nereye?	*where?* (indicates movement so 'where to?')
birinci*	*first*
ikinci*	*second*
liman	*port*
sahil	*coast*
merkez	*centre*
rica ederim	*not at all*

*In the spoken language **birinci / birincisi** and **ikinci / ikincisi** are used interchangeably.

Language points

Endings showing position or movement

-de, -da *at / on / in*

Remember we covered the Turkish noun ending -de in Unit 4. It has two variations (-de and -da) and shows there is no movement to, or from, and it means *at, on* or *in*.

-e, -a *to*

The ending -e, which has two variations (-e and -a) and indicates there is movement towards, and means *to*. The endings follow the same principle as -de and -da.

- -a harmonizes best with **a, ı, o, u**
- -e harmonizes best with **e, i, ö, ü**

Here are some examples:

İstanbul'*a*	*to Istanbul*
Türkiye'*ye*	*to Turkey*
Ankara'*ya*	*to Ankara*
Müzeye	*to the museum*

Connecting *y*

In Turkish you cannot put two vowels next to each other within a word as it makes pronunciation difficult. If a word ends in a vowel and the ending starts with a vowel, insert the consonant -y- between them, e.g. not **müzee** but **müzeye**. This makes the word more pronounceable.

-den, -dan *from*

The ending **-den**, which has two variations (**-den** and **-dan**) means *from*, in the sense of movement away from.

İngiltere'*den*	*from England*
Amerika'*dan*	*from America*
Saray*dan* camiye	*from the palace to the mosque*
Müze*den* meydan*a*	*from the museum to the square*

Remember, most proper nouns (names of places and people) have an apostrophe before the ending.

ℹ Istanbul is the only city in the world built on two continents – Europe and Asia. It stands on the shore of the **Istanbul Boğazı** *Bosporus* where the waters of the **Karadeniz** *Black Sea* merge with those of the **Marmara Denizi** *Sea of Marmara* and **Haliç** *the Golden Horn*. Here on this splendid site Istanbul guards the precious relics of the three empires of which she has been the capital; a unique link between East and West, past and present.

Istanbul has infinite variety: **müzeler** *museums*, **tarihi kiliseler** *ancient churches*, **saraylar** *palaces*, **muhteşem camiler** *great mosques*, **Kapalı Çarşı** *covered market* and the **Istanbul Boğazı** *Bosporus*.

A stay in Istanbul is not complete without the traditional and unforgettable excursion by boat along the **Bosporus**. The shore is lined with modern hotels, **yalılar** *old wooden villas*, **mermer saraylar** *marble palaces*, **hisarlar** *fortresses*, and **küçük balıkçı köyleri** *small fishing villages*. The best and most relaxing way to see the **Bosporus** is to board one of the **yolcu vapuru** *passenger boats* that regularly zigzag along the shores starting from **Eminönü** and stopping alternately on the **Asya** *Asian* and **Avrupa** *European* sides. **Gidiş-Dönüş** *the round trip* takes about six hours and the fare is very reasonable.

In 21st-century Turkish 'Istanbul' can be spelled in two different ways: **İstanbul** (dotted capital 'I') and **Istanbul** (undotted capital 'I'). Both forms are correct, but in this book we've chosen to use the spelling with the dotted 'İ' whenever we refer to the name of the city in Turkish.

Practice

1 Can you match the following traffic signs with their meanings below?

a

i Sola dön.

b

ii Dur.

c

iii Düz git.

d

iv Sağa dön.

2 Match the following questions with their answers.

a İçkiler kimden?   i Evet, Sultan Ahmet Meydanı'nda.
b Kahveler senden mi?   ii Vanessa'dan.
c Posta kartı kimden?   iii Benden.
d Istanbul nerede?   iv Türkiye'de.
e Ayasofya Istanbul'da mı?   v Hayır, senden.

3 Write down the meanings of the following Turkish phrases.

a Buyurun.
b Benden.
c Rahatsız etmeyin!
d Afedersiniz.
e Özür dilerim.
f Bilmiyorum.
g Teşekkürler.
h Rica ederim.

4 Here are some public signs with formal endings. Where would you see them?

a İtiniz.
b Çekiniz.
c Kart kullanınız.
d İstanbul'a Hoş Geldiniz.
e Yavaş sürünüz.
f Sağı takip ediniz.

i   on a door
ii on an escalator
iii on a door
iv on a road sign
v   on a public telephone
vi approaching Istanbul

▶ **5** Look at the map of Turkey below showing the distances from Istanbul to other cities in Turkey. Write the answers first, then listen and repeat them. For help with the numbers, see Units 2 and 3.

a İstanbul'dan Ankara'ya kaç km?
b İstanbul'dan Bodrum'a kaç km?
c İstanbul'dan Çanakkale'ye kaç km?
d İstanbul'dan Safranbolu'ya kaç km?
e İstanbul'dan Pamukkale'ye kaç km?
f İstanbul'dan Marmaris'e kaç km?
g İstanbul'dan Göreme'ye kaç km?
h İstanbul'dan İzmir'e kaç km?
i İstanbul'dan Trabzon'a kaç km?
j İstanbul'dan Fethiye'ye kaç km?

6 Translate these sentences into English. Look up the vocabulary in this unit or use your dictionary.

a Danışma nerede?
b Işıkları geçin.
c Düz gidin, sağda birinci yola dönün.
d Düz gidin, solda, köşede.

 7

Listen to the recording of the routes of the Blue Cruises and stops while looking at the map. Then put the necessary endings on the following place names e.g. **-den**, **-dan** (*from*), **-e**, **-a** (*to*).

a *Birinci gün*   *Marmaris – Çiftlik*
b *İkinci gün*   *Çiftlik – Bozukkale*

c *Üçüncü gün*   *Bozukkale – Aktur – Datça*
d *Dördüncü gün*   *Datça – Knidos*
e *Beşinci gün*   *Knidos – Bodrum*

Note: **d** becomes **t** after these consonants: **ç, f, h, k, p, s, ş, t**. But don't worry too much about consonant changes at this stage.

▶ **8 Pronunciation: j, k, l.** Don't worry about the meanings of the words, just listen to the pronunciation and then repeat.

j	k	l
jip	ak	al
jet	iki	el
jilet	kar	la
jeton	kim	bal

▶ Mini-test

Well done; you have now completed Unit 5! Now you will be able to ask for, give and understand directions in Turkish, you will be able to get around new places and clarify meanings. Give yourself a point for each of the following questions that you answer correctly in Turkish.

1 Ask for directions to the bank.
2 Ask where the taxis are.
3 Tell a taxi driver to go straight on and turn right at the corner.
4 Ask when the museum is open.
5 Ask for two tickets.

Points:_____/5

06

I like the weather here!

In this unit you will learn
- how to talk about the weather
- how to compare months and seasons
- how to talk about your likes and dislikes
- pronunciation: **m, n, o**

▶ Dialogue 1 At a travel agency

Anne and her partner are at a travel agency looking for a suitable holiday destination.

Listen to, or read at least twice, this dialogue about the weather.

Anne   Türkiye'de nereleri sıcak?
Travel agent Güney, ağustos ve temmuzda çok sıcak. İlkbaharda ılık, haziranda sıcak.
Anne   Biz çok sıcak seviyoruz. Yağmur sevmiyoruz. Çocuklar da denizi ve kumu seviyor.

The travel agent looks at the average temperatures for various places in Turkey.

Travel agent Temmuzda Alanya 26°C, Antalya 28°C, Bodrum 27°C, Fethiye 27°C, İstanbul 23°C. Temmuzda, en sıcak Antalya. Yazın güneyde hiç yağmur yok. Hava hep güneşli. İlkbaharda daha çok bahar yağmurları ve sonra da gökkuşağı vardır. Kırlarda kır çiçekleri çok çeşitli ve güzeldir.
Anne   Evet. Antalya'ya hangi günler uçak var?

*The travel agent looks at the computer (**bilgisayar**) flight timetable.*

Travel agent Pazartesi, çarşamba, cuma günde bir uçak. Cumartesi ve pazar günde iki uçak var.
Anne   5 mayıs pazar günü yer var mı?
Travel agent Evet, var. Kaç kişilik?

ℹ If you want to check flight information yourself, you may find the Turkish Airlines (THY) website useful:
http://www3.thy.com//troyaonline/timetable.tk?lang=en

Questions

Read the dialogue and answer these questions:

1 Türkiye'de nereleri sıcak?
2 Temmuzda en sıcak neresi?
3 Antalya'ya hangi günler uçak var?

Türkiye	Turkey
nereler?	what places?
sıcak	hot
güney	south
ağustos	August
temmuz	July
ilkbahar	spring
ılık	warm
haziran	June
seviyoruz	we like / love
yağmur	rain
sevmiyoruz	we do not like / love
çocuklar	children
deniz	sea
kum	sand
en	the most (-est)
en sıcak	hottest
hava	weather
yaz	summer
güneşli	sunny
daha çok	mostly
daha	more (-er)
sonra	then
gökkuşağı	rainbow
kır	countryside / wild
kır çiçekleri	wild flowers
çeşitli	various
güzel	beautiful
gün	day
pazartesi	Monday
çarşamba	Wednesday
cuma	Friday
cumartesi	Saturday
pazar	Sunday
uçak	aeroplane
mayıs	May
yer	place / seat
kaç kişilik?	for how many people?

Language points

Points of the compass

▶ The four seasons

Listen, then repeat.

ilkbahar	*spring*
yaz	*summer*
sonbahar	*autumn / fall*
kış	*winter*

To say *in spring* etc.:

ilkbaharda	*in spring*
yazın	*in summer*
sonbaharda	*in autumn*
kışın	*in winter*

▶ The months of the year

Listen, then repeat.

ocak	*January*	**temmuz**	*July*
şubat	*February*	**ağustos**	*August*
mart	*March*	**eylül**	*September*
nisan	*April*	**ekim**	*October*
mayıs	*May*	**kasım**	*November*
haziran	*June*	**aralık**	*December*

To say *in June*, etc., you add the **-de** or **-da** ending, according to vowel harmony:

hazıranda   *in June*

▶ The days of the week

Listen, then repeat.

pazar (günü)	*Sunday*
pazartesi (günü)	*Monday*
salı (günü)	*Tuesday*
çarşamba (günü)	*Wednesday*
perşembe (günü)	*Thursday*
cuma (günü)	*Friday*
cumartesi (günü)	*Saturday*

On Monday, on Tuesday, etc. is translated by **pazartesi günü, salı günü**.

Capital letters

Unlike English, Turkish does not use capital letters for the days of the week and months of the year unless they are important dates or special days.

For example, in the sentence **her pazar çok uyuyorum** *every Sunday I sleep a lot* you can see that there is no capital letter for **pazar**. However, when writing about 1st May, which is the Spring Festival, a capital letter is used: **1 Mayıs**.

1 Mayıs Bahar Bayramı'dır.   *1st May is the Spring Festival.*

Dates

Writing or saying dates is very easy. Simply say the number followed by the month:

bir mayıs   *1 May*
yirmi iki şubat   *22 February*

Years are said just like reading a number, so the year 2222 would be **iki bin iki yüz yirmi iki** *two thousand two hundred twenty-two*.

-dır (-dir, -dur, -dür): formal 'is'

There is no equivalent of the English word *is*. So the Turkish sentence **Ev kırmızı** means 'The house is red', but it actually says 'House red'. However, when people want to sound very formal, they use the ending **-dir**. You would not commonly use this ending in conversation, but you need to recognize it when you see it, usually on official notices, in official documents and in newspaper articles.

Durmak Yasaktır.	*Stopping is forbidden.*
Geçmek Yasaktır.	*Crossing / passing is forbidden.*
Türkler'in dili Türkçe'dir.	*The language of Turks is Turkish.*

More examples can be found in *Teach Yourself Turkish* (Unit 7).

Another use of **-dir** is for describing unchanging facts:

Güney Türkiye'de yazlar çok sıcaktır.	*In south Turkey summers are very hot.*

You will also notice that **d** changes to **t** after **k**. For more examples look at Unit 9 and *Teach Yourself Turkish* (Unit 3). At this stage it is not important to remember to make this change but it is important to recognize it when you see it.

More about word endings

In Turkish, certain verbs take certain endings. This is similar to the way in which some English verbs are followed by a preposition, as *out* and *on* in *to get out*, *to get on*. Good dictionaries give these endings next to the verb. The best way of learning the endings is step by step; when you learn a new verb look at the previous word to see if there is an ending and if so, try to remember it.

Some verbs do not take any endings. At this stage just pay attention; you could make a note or highlight the ending and the verb in the book to help you to remember it. For example, **sevmek** *to love* takes the **-ı** (**-i, -u, -ü**) direct object ending:

Biz yazı seviyoruz.	*We love summers* (i.e. *We love the summer*).
Biz güneşi çok seviyoruz.	*We love the sun.*
Biz yağmuru sevmiyoruz.	*We do not like / love the rain.*

In these examples, *summer*, *sun* and *rain* are the objects of the verb *to love*.

When a personal pronoun (I, you, he, etc.) is the direct object of a verb, you give it an -i ending. This is because personal pronouns stand for *specific* things or people.

Biz seni seviyoruz.   *We love you.*

The following table shows the personal pronouns with -i endings.

Personal pronoun		with *-i* (*-ı, -u, -ü*) ending	
ben	*I*	**beni**	*me*
sen	*you*	**seni**	*you*
o	*he, she, it*	**onu**	*him, her, it*
biz	*we*	**bizi**	*us*
siz	*you*	**sizi**	*you*
onlar	*they*	**onları**	*them*

Comparisons

In English there are two ways to say *more* and *most*: with short words -er or -est are added (*nice, nicer, the nicest*), and with longer words *more* and *most* are used (*beautiful, more beautiful, the most beautiful*). In Turkish, you just have one system to learn.

daha *more (-er)*

The word **daha** is put before the adjective:

daha sıcak   *hotter / warmer*
Bugün hava daha sıcak.   *The weather is hotter today.*
                          (lit. *Today weather hotter.*)
daha güzel   *more beautiful*

Then, to make the comparison, for *than*, you add the ending -den, -dan, -ten, -tan to the adjective:

Bugün hava dünden daha   *Today the weather is warmer*
  sıcak.   *than yesterday.*
Temmuzda hava hazirandan *The weather in July is warmer*
  daha sıcak.   *than in June.* (lit. *In July weather from/than June hotter.*)

İstanbul Ankara ve İzmir'den *Istanbul is bigger than Ankara*
  daha büyük.   *and Izmir.* (lit. *Istanbul Ankara and Izmir from/than bigger.*)

En *the most (-est)*

The word **en** is put before the adjective:

en sıcak	*the warmest (hottest)*
Rize en yağmurlu.	*Rize is the rainiest.*
	(lit. Rize most rainy/rainiest.)

Making adjectives using *-li (-lı, -lu, -lü)* endings

By putting -li or its variations on the end of a noun it is very easy
to make an adjective. Simply, the ending -li means *with*.

Hava nasıl? *What is the weather like?*

• güneş *sun*

Bugün hava güneşli.
Today it is sunny.

• bulut *cloud*

Bugün hava bulutlu.
Today it is cloudy.

• yağmur *rain*

Bugün hava yağmurlu.
Today it is raining.

sis *fog*

Bugün hava sisli.
Today it is foggy.

kar *snow*

Bugün hava karlı.
Today it is snowy.

rüzgar *wind*

Bugün hava rüzgarlı.
Today it is windy.

ⓘ Special days

The followings are all important dates in the Turkish calendar. Why not put the dates, days of the week and the months of the year in your diary in Turkish?

Fixed public holidays *Bayramlar* ☾*

1 Ocak	Yılbaşı	*New Year's Day*
23 Nisan	Çocuk Bayramı	*National Sovereignty and Children's Day*
19 Mayıs	Gençlik ve Spor Bayramı	*Atatürk Commemoration and Youth and Sports Day*
30 Ağustos	Zafer Bayramı	*Victory Day*
29 Ekim	Cumhuriyet Bayramı	*Republic Day*

Moveable Islamic public holidays (*

| 14 Kasım 2004 | Ramazan/Şeker Bayramı | *Ramadan / End of the Fast* |
| 2 Şubat 2004 | Kurban Bayramı | *Helping the poor* |

Non-holiday celebration

| 1 Mayıs | Bahar Bayramı | *Spring Festival* |
| Mayısın 2nci Pazar günü | Anneler günü | *Mother's Day* |

During the month of **Ramazan** *Ramadan* practising Muslims do not eat or drink between sunrise and sunset. In traditional areas, you will find that restaurants will not open until sunset, but in tourist areas you will find that places to eat and drink are open as usual during daylight areas even during **Ramazan**. If you are not Muslim – don't worry, you are not expected to fast!

However, as a way of respect you may decide not to eat or drink too overtly. At sunset during **Ramazan** there is an air of celebration as people come together to break their fast. The dates of **Ramazan** change each year, as they are set by the lunar calendar. At the end of the fasting month there is a national holiday, **Şeker Bayramı**, which is a time of celebration when families get together.

◨ Dialogue 2 We like different things

Some young people are sitting at a seaside café in the shade of a willow tree by the sea. Listen to, or read the dialogue at least twice. Listen out for the answers to these questions:

Questions

1 What do the boys like?
2 What do the girls like?

Cem	Ben ve Gökhan futbol, basketbol, voleybol ve tenis seviyoruz.
Gökhan	Ama en çok futbolu.
Vanessa	Biz denizi ve dansı, günlük gezileri seviyoruz. Yağmursuz ve rüzgarsız ne güzel bir gün!
Cem	Annemler de günlük gezileri, özellikle harabeleri gezmeyi seviyor. Restoranlarda yemek yemek çok keyifli. (*To a*

friend standing in the sun): Orada durma, çok güneş var, gölgeye gel. (*He calls out to the waiter to order some ice cream*) Garson, bana bir çikolatalı dondurma.

They all order different flavours of ice cream.

Vanessa	Bana sade dondurma.
Cem	Bana meyveli.
Çiğdem	Bana limonlu.
Gökhan	Bana da karışık.
Garson	Tamam, efendim.

Questions

Read the dialogue again and answer the following questions.

3 Nasıl bir gün?
4 Restoranlarda yemek yemek keyifli mi?
5 Kaç çeşit dondurma?

futbol	*football*
basketbol	*basketball*
voleybol	*volleyball*
tenis	*tennis*
dans	*dance*
günlük	*daily (day)*
gezi	*trip / journey*
yağmursuz	*without rain*
rüzgarsız	*without wind*
annemler	*my parents* (lit. *my mothers*)
özellikle	*especially*
harabe	*ruin*
gezmek	*travel / trip*
yemek yemek	*to eat food* (see **Language points**)
keyifli	*joyous, pleasurable*
orada	*there*
gölge	*shade*
dondurma	*ice cream*
çikolatalı	*chocolate flavoured / with chocolate*
sade	*plain / vanilla flavour*
meyveli	*fruit flavoured / with fruit*
limonlu	*lemon flavoured*
karışık	*mixed*

Language points

yemek yemek *to eat food*

In Turkish there are a handful of verbs which behave in a special way. They are fairly common verbs, so it is worth taking the time to learn them! For example, in Turkish, you can't just 'eat' – you have to eat *something*, e.g. **salata yemek** *to eat salad*. If you don't want to specify what's being eaten, you have to say **yemek yemek**. These words look the same, but the first one is the noun, and the second one is the verb. Other examples include:

uyku uyumak	*to sleep (to sleep a sleep)*
yazı yazmak	*to write (to write a writing)*
oyun oynamak	*to play (to play a game)*

-sız (-siz, -suz, -süz) *without*

This ending means **without** and it is the opposite of **-li** ending which means *with*. You can put it on the end of nouns to make some more adjectives. (It follows **i**-type vowel harmony.)

güneş*siz*	*without sun*
bulut*suz*	*without cloud*
yağmur*suz*	*without rain*
kar*sız*	*without snow*

Now you know how to make two different adjectives from each noun!

annemler *my parents*

Anne means *mother*. **Annemler** in plural form implies *my mother and my father*. **Ayşeler** means *Ayşe and her family*. This is similar to the expression *the Browns* in English. But in Turkish the first names, or the titles, are used instead of the surnames and this practice is informal.

-me, -ma *don't*

To tell people not to do things, add **-me** or **-ma** to the end of an informal command. For formal negative commands, add **-in** or **-iniz** to the informal negative (**-iniz** is very formal). For example:

Infinitive	Informal negative command	Polite (formal) negative commands	
durmak *to stop*	durma *don't stop*	durmayın	durmayınız
geçmek *to cross*	geçme *don't cross*	geçmeyin	geçmeyiniz

-me or -ma comes after the verbs, not after the nouns or adjectives. Remember that **değil** is used to make adjectives or nouns negative.

Reading comprehension

Read the passage about the seasons and climate in Turkey. Then answer the questions at the end of the text using **doğru** *true* or **yanlış** *false*.

Türkiye'de mevsimler ve iklim

Türkiye'de dört mevsim vardır ve bunlar ilkbahar, yaz, sonbahar, kıştır. İklim de her bölgede çok farklıdır.

Akdeniz, Ege ve Marmara'da yazlar sıcak ve kurak, kışlar ılık ve yağmurludur. Çok yüksek dağlarda kar vardır. Türkiye'de deniz kenarları daha ılıktır. Istanbul ve Marmara'da kışlar ortalama 4°C, yazlar 27°C.

Karadeniz'de yazlar sıcaktır. Kışlar güneyden daha serindir. Ara sıra don ve her mevsimde kar vardır. Yazlar 23°C ve kışlar 7°C dır. En çok yağmur Rize'dedir.

Orta Anadolu'da gece ve gündüz arasında sıcaklık çok farklıdır. Yazlar daha az sıcaktır. Ortalama sıcaklık yazlarda 23°C , kışlarda –2°C. Güneydoğu Anadolu'da yazlar çok sıcak kışlar daha az soğuktur.

Doğu Anadolu'da kışlar çok soğuk, karlı ve uzundur. Yazlar yağmursuzdur. Türkiye'de en soğuk yerler kuzey doğudur.

Güney'de kumda iken Toroslar'da kar vardır.

mevsim	*season*
iklim	*climate*
bölge	*region*
farklı	*different*
Akdeniz	*Mediterranean*
Ege	*Aegean*

Marmara	*Marmara* (the sea and region)
kurak	*dry*
yüksek	*high*
dağ	*mountain*
deniz kenarları	*seaside*
ortalama	*average*
Karadeniz	*the Black Sea*
serin	*cool*
ara sıra	*sometimes*
don	*frost*
arasında	*between*
Anadolu	*Anatolia*
uzundur	*it is long*
iken	*while / when*

True or false?

1 En sıcak mevsim yazdır.
2 Türkiye'de üç mevsim vardır.
3 İstanbul'da kışlar ortalama 4°C.
4 En çok yağmur Ankara'dadır.
5 Orta Anadolu'da Yazın gece ve gündüz sıcaklık farklıdır.
6 Türkiye'de en sıcak yer Doğu Anadolu'dur.

Practice

▶ 1 Look at the map of Turkey and write down where these places are, using the points of the compass. Then repeat what the speaker says on the recording.

The first one has been done for you:

a İzmir nerede?   *Answer*: **batıda**

a İzmir nerede?
b İstanbul nerede?
c Ankara nerede?
d Van nerede?
e Bodrum nerede?
f Samsun nerede?
g Mersin nerede?
h Alanya nerede?
i Marmaris nerede?

2 Match the words with the corresponding pictures.

a güneşli
b bulutlu
c yağmurlu
d karlı
e sisli
f sıcak
g soğuk

i

ii

iii

iv

v

vi

vii

3 Can you work out the answer to this puzzle?

Ali Betül'den daha uzun boylu, ama Ali Can'dan daha kısa boylu. Dursun Betül'den daha kısa boylu. En kısa boylu kim?

4 Fill in the blanks to give months of the year:

a a _ us _ _ s
b _ yl _ l
c _ _ i _
d h _ zi _ _ n
e te _ _ u _
f _ ub _ t

▶ 5 **Pronunciation: m, n, o.** First, listen without looking; second, listen while looking at the sounds below; finally listen and repeat. Do not worry about the meaning.

m	n	o
em	an	on
ma	no	do
Cem	ön	ol
güm	kin	çok

6 Wordsearch. Find ten words connected to the weather.

F	A	G	H	A	V	A	Y	U	P
S	İ	S	L	İ	F	H	A	O	S
I	B	H	P	S	E	O	Ğ	P	O
C	E	K	L	R	Z	G	M	O	Ğ
A	Ç	I	K	A	V	A	U	Y	U
K	A	R	L	I	G	Y	R	T	K
A	D	B	U	L	U	T	L	U	S
C	R	D	D	R	S	P	U	L	E
G	Ü	N	E	Ş	L	İ	S	Y	F
H	R	Ü	Z	G	A	R	L	I	R

▶ Mini-test

Well done; you have now completed Unit 6! Now you will be able to talk about the weather, seasons, months of the year, days of the week, and make comparisons. Give yourself a point for each of the following statements or questions that you can say in Turkish.

1 Say there is no rain in summer.
2 Say that it rains in spring.
3 Say that July is hotter than February.
4 Say you like dancing and volleyball the most.
5 Ask what day there are flights to Bodrum.
6 Order a fruit-flavoured ice cream.

Points:_____/6

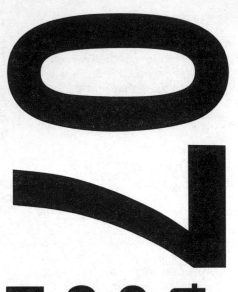

07

talking about oneself and describing people

In this unit you will learn
- how to talk about yourself (*I am …*)
- how to ask other people about themselves (are you …?)
- how to describe yourself and other people
- more about addressing people correctly
- how to increase your word power with a few simple word endings
- pronunciation: ö, p, r

▶ Dialogue 1 Where are you from?

Two passengers on a flight to Istanbul strike up a conversation. Listen to the dialogue a couple of times and try to answer the following questions. Next, read the dialogue, listen to it again and try to answer the questions at the end of the dialogue.

Questions

1 Where is she from?
2 Where is he from?

Woman	Merhaba.
Man	Merhaba.
Woman	Nerelisin?
Man	Leeds'liyim. Ya siz nerelisiniz?
Woman	Ben Almanım. Bonn'luyum.
Man	Ben İngilizim ama eşim Türk, İstanbul'lu. (*The man holds up a book.*) Bu kitap Türkçe öğrenmek için, *Teach Yourself Turkish.* Ben hem Türkçe hem de Almanca, Fransızca, İspanyolca, İtalyanca ve biraz da Bulgarca biliyorum. Türkler'i, Türkçe'yi ve Türkiye'yi çok seviyorum. Kızımız Vanessa da Türkçe biliyor.
Woman	Gerçekten mi? Çok ilginç.
Man	Tatillerde Türkiye'ye gitmek çok keyifli. Biz çok şanslıyız. Türkler çok samimi ve dürüst, değil mi?
Woman	Evet, haklısınız.

Questions

3 Erkek Türk mü, İngiliz mi?
4 Erkek hangi dilleri biliyor?
5 Kim Türkçe biliyor?

Nerelisin?	*Where are you from?*
eşim	*my wife / my husband* (my spouse)
Türkçe	*Turkish* (language)
Almanca	*German* (language)
Fransızca	*French* (language)
İspanyolca	*Spanish* (language)
İtalyanca	*Italian* (language)
Bulgarca	*Bulgarian* (language)
biliyorum	*I know*
kızımız	*our daughter*
seviyorum	*I like*

gerçekten	really
ilginç	interesting
tatil	holiday
keyifli	enjoyable
şans	chance / luck
samimi	friendly
dürüst	honest
haklısınız	you are right

Language points

Word power

You have already learnt some nouns, adjectives and verbs. Now if you learn some more word endings you will find that your vocabulary and ability to communicate will rapidly increase!

The verb 'to be'

The verb **to be** (*am, is, are*) is very useful. It can be used with nouns, adjectives and pronouns to describe yourself and others. In Turkish, as in many languages, the verb *to be* does not have an exact equivalent. In Turkish there are no separate words for *am, is, are*, etc. Instead **-im, -sin, -iz, -siniz** and **-ler** are added to the end of adjectives, nouns or pronouns. Once you have learnt these endings you can add them to adjectives, nouns and pronouns you already know, and you will find that you can make a huge number of new sentences very easily and quickly.

Singular	Plural
ben**im** *I am*	biz**iz** *we are*
sen**sin** *you are (informal)*	siz**siniz** *you are* (formal / plural)
o *he /she / it is*	on**lar** *they are*

Here are some examples of adjectives of nationality with the appropriate endings, showing vowel harmony:

ben	İngiliz**im**	İspanyol**um**	Türk**üm**	Alman**ım**
sen	İngiliz**sin**	İspanyol**sun**	Türk**sün**	Alman**sın**
o	İngiliz*	İspanyol*	Türk*	Alman*

biz	İngiliziz	İspanyoluz	Türküz	Almanız
siz	İngilizsiniz	İspanyolsunuz	Türksünüz	Almansınız
onlar	İngiliz(ler)	İspanyol(lar)	Türk(ler)	Alman(lar)

*i.e. no ending

Most adjectives follow the pattern above, but the letter y is added when the root word ends in a vowel and the personal ending starts with a vowel. This makes the word easier to pronounce. Letters inserted like this are called buffer consonants. Here is an example of 'buffer y' being used:

Amerikalıyız. *We are American.*
Amerikalıyım. *I am American.*

Countries, nationalities and languages

Kıtalar ve memleketler *Continents and countries*	Milliyetler *Nationalities*	Diller *Languages*	Başkentler *Capitals*
Almanya *Germany*	Alman	Almanca	Berlin
Avrupa *Europe*	Avrupalı		
Asya *Asia*	Asyalı		
Amerika *United States of America*	Amerikalı / Amerikan	İngilizce	Washington
Avustralya *Australia*	Avustralyalı	İngilizce	Canberra
Büyük Britanya *Great Britain*	British	İngilizce / Galce	Londra
Belçika *Belgium*	Belçikalı	Fransızca / Hollandaca	Brüksel
Fransa *France*	Fransız	Fransızca	Paris
İngiltere *England*	İngiliz	İngilizce	Londra
İrlanda *Ireland*	İrlandalı	İrlandaca	Dublin
İspanya *Spain*	İspanyol	İspanyolca	Madrid
Japonya *Japan*	Japon	Japonca	Tokyo
Kanada *Canada*	Kanadalı	İngilizce / Fransızca	Ottawa
İskoçya *Scotland*	İskoç	İskoçça	Edinburg
Türkiye *Turkey*	Türk	Türkçe	Ankara
Galler *Wales*	Galli	Galce	Kardif

▶ Dialogue 2 Are you Turkish?

Two young women are sitting next to each other on the coach (**otobüs**) to Ankara. They introduce themselves and begin to chat.

Listen to the dialogue a couple of times and see if you can answer the following questions. Read the dialogue, listen to it

again then try to answer the questions at the end of the
dialogue.

Questions

1 Is Ayda Turkish or American?
2 Who is a model?

Susie Merhaba, ben Susie. Ya sen?
Ayda Ben Ayda.
Susie Türk müsün?
Ayda Evet. Ya sen? Amerikalı mısın?
Susie Hayır. İngilizim. Londralıyım.
Ayda Manken misin?
Susie Hayır, öğrenciyim. Ya sen?
Ayda Ben doktorum.
Susie Çok akıllısın.
Ayda Çok akıllı değilim ama çok çalışkanım.
Susie Evli misin?
Ayda Hayır, nişanlıyım. Sen?
Susie Ben bekarım, henüz 23 yaşındayım. Nişanlın yakışıklı mı?
*(Ayda takes out a photograph of her fiancé from her wallet and
describes him to Susie.)*
Ayda Cem uzun boylu, esmer, siyah saçlı, siyah gözlü ve tabii
bence çok yakışıklı. Çok akıllı ve iyi bir insan. Mühendis ve
biz çok iyi arkadaşız.

Questions

3 Susie Amerikalı mı, İngiliz mi?
4 Susie manken mi, öğrenci mi?
5 Kim doktor?
6 Cem yakışıklı mı? Cem nasıl?

model	*model*
öğrenci	*student*
doktor	*doctor*
akıllı	*clever*
çalışkan	*hard working*
evli	*married*
nişanlı	*engaged*
bekar	*single*
henüz	*only*

x yaşındayım	I'm x years old
nişanlın	your fiancé
yakışıklı	handsome
uzun boylu	tall
esmer	dark / olive skinned
siyah saçlı	black haired
siyah gözlü	dark-brown eyed (lit. black eyed)
tabii	of course
bence	in my opinion
insan	person
mühendis	engineer
arkadaş	friend

Language points

You have already seen how the verb *to be* is used with adjectives such as nationalities. The verb *to be* can also be used with nouns. In Dialogue 2 you saw the endings of the verb *to be* used with the names of jobs.

Here is an example of a noun **sekreter** *secretary* with the personal endings added:

Sekreter**im**.	*I am a secretary.*
Sekreter**sin**.	*You are a secretary.*
Sekreter.	*He / she is a secretary.*
Sekreter**iz**.	*We are secretaries.*
Sekreter**siniz**.	*You are secretaries.*
Sekreter**ler**.	*They are secretaries.*

The following table provides examples of some other jobs to show vowel harmony:

	Öğretmen *teacher*	**Doktor** *doctor*	**Profesör** *professor*	**Bakkal** *grocer*
ben	öğretmen**im**	doktor**um**	profesör**üm**	bakkal**ım**
sen	öğretmen**sin**	doktor**sun**	profesör**sün**	bakkal**sın**
o	öğretmen	doktor	profesör	bakkal
biz	öğretmen**iz**	doktor**uz**	profesör**üz**	bakkal**ız**
siz	öğretmen**siniz**	doktor**sunuz**	profesör**sünüz**	bakkal**sınız**
onlar	öğretmen**(ler)**	doktor**(lar)**	profesör**(ler)**	bakkal**(lar)**

All of the endings for the verb *to be*, except the *they* form (**-ler** ending), follow the rules of vowel harmony. At this stage, do not worry about getting the harmony right, just have a go – Turkish people will understand you, even if you make some mistakes. Making mistakes is a natural part of the language learning process! Don't wait till you know the language perfectly before trying to have a conversation – Turkish people will appreciate it if you have a go, no matter how little you know.

In Turkish, you will come across simple verbless sentences, e.g. **Doktor.** (*He or she is a doctor.*), **Çalışkan.** (*She / he / it is hard working*). You do not usually use the personal pronouns (**ben, sen,** etc.) when using the verb *to be* endings (**im, sin,** etc.) unless you want to make the point strongly. For example, **ben öğretmenim,** *I am a teacher **not you**.* You use the personal pronouns if you want to emphasize the point. You can see that in Turkish a few words can convey a great deal of meaning. You may be wondering how you will know whether **öğretmen** means *he is a teacher* or *she is a teacher*, but this will usually be clear from the context – you will normally know who you are having a conversation about!

▶ Dialogue 3 How are you?

Listen to the conversation on the recording a couple times and then read the dialogue, listen to it again and answer the questions at the end of the dialogue.

Ülkü telephones her good friend Gonca.

Ülkü   Alo!
Gonca   Alo. Ülkü, sen misin?
Ülkü   Benim. Gonca Abla, siz misiniz?
Gonca   Benim canım. Nasılsın?
Ülkü   Teşekkür ederim, iyiyim. Siz nasılsınız?
Gonca   Ben de iyiyim.

Questions

1 Ülkü nasıl?
2 Gonca nasıl?

| benim | *it's me* | canım | *my dear* |

i Social or affectionate closeness between people is expressed by using the names of family relations. If one person calls another **amca** *uncle*, **abla** *elder sister*, **abi** *elder brother*, **teyze** *auntie*, it does not necessarily mean that they are related. In Dialogue 3, you heard Ülkü refer to her friend as **Gonca abla**, which shows affection and respect for an older person. (For more details see *Teach Yourself Turkish*, Unit 4.) The same family terms are used to indicate that there is no sexual motive when talking to someone of the opposite sex, that one's intentions are purely innocent and family-like. It is quite acceptable for a young man sitting on a bus to call over to an older woman **abla gel otur** *older / big sister, come and sit down*.

Language points

Canım *My dear*

Canım means literally *my soul*, but it is used as an affectionate term to mean *my dear*. You heard Gonca refer to Ülkü as **canım** in the previous dialogue. Another way of expressing the same feeling is to add the ending **-ciğim** after a loved one's name or title. For example, **Canım Cem'ciğim** *my dear dear Cem*, **Anneciğim** *my dear Mum*.

ben / benim; -im *I am / my*

When added to the end of nouns and adjectives the ending **-im** (**-ım, -um, -üm**) can mean *my*.

Tık tık.	*Knock knock.*
Kim o?	*Who is it / that?*
Benim, canım.	*(I) It's me (my) dear.*

When a mother cuddles her daughter she might say **canım benim** or **Benim canım** *my dear*.

Ben öğretmenim.	*I am a teacher.*
Benim öğretmenim.	*My teacher.*
Ben güzelim.	*I am beautiful.*
Benim güzelim.	*My beauty.*

In colloquial conversations, however, these endings are not used, e.g. **Merhaba, ben Şafak** would be used instead of **Ben Şafak'ım**.

Ben benim, sen sensin, biz farklıyız would be translated as *I am who I am (this is me), you are who you are (this is you), we are different.*

▶ Dialogue 4 Hello?

Listen to the recording a few times and answer the question.

Şafak telephones Banu. They are cousins and talk very informally.

Banu	Alo?
Şafak	Merhaba, Banu, ben Şafak.
Banu	Merhaba, Şafak. Nasılsın?
Şafak	İyiyim.

Question

Şafak nasıl?

ℹ️ Although Banu and Şafak don't do it here, it is common to shorten first names in friendly, intimate situations, e.g. **Şaf** for **Şafak**, **Asu** for **Asuman** in the same way as in English *David* is shortened to *Dave*. Sometimes you will also hear an **ş** added to the end of names to give a similar affectionate and friendly tone, e.g. **Aloş** for **Ali**, **Banuş** for **Banu**.

Language points

Word power

Turkish takes a word and changes the meaning by adding endings. Small parts of words are used to build up meaning. At this stage in the book, you have already learnt some nouns, adjectives and verbs. If you now learn some of the word endings, which are the main building blocks of Turkish, you will find that you can use just a few nouns, adjectives and verbs to create lots of new meanings easily. You will also be able to take a good guess at the meanings of new words which you meet. Your word power will increase rapidly!

Saying 'I'm not' – negatives with the verb 'to be'

We have already learnt that **değil** means *not*. It can be used with a noun or adjective to make a negative sentence. For the negative of *to be*, the noun or adjective is unchanged and the personal endings are added to the word **değil**, which goes at the end of the sentence.

Değil-**im**	Ben bakkal değil**im**.	*I am not a grocer.*
Değil-**sin**	Sen bakkal değil**sin**.	*You are not a grocer.*
Değil	O bakkal değil.	*He / She is not a grocer.*
Değil-**iz**	Biz bakkal değil**iz**.	*We are not grocers.*
Değil-**siniz**	Siz bakkal değil**siniz**.	*You are not grocers.*
Değil-**ler**	Onlar bakkal değil(**ler**)	*They are not grocers.*

Asking 'Am I ...?' 'Are you ...?' – making questions with the verb 'to be'

For questions using the verb *to be*, the adjective or noun does not change and the personal endings are added to the **mı-, mi-, mu-, mü-** question words which you learnt in Unit 4. When written, the two words are separate but when they are spoken they are said as one word.

Ben **mi**?	*Is it me?*		Biz **mi**?	*Is it us?*
Sen **mi**?	*Is it you?*		Siz **mi**?	*Is it you?*
O **mu**?	*Is it him / her / it?*		Onlar **mı**?	*Is it them?*

Sekreter **miyim**?	*Am I a secretary?*
Öğretmen **misin**?	*Are you a secretary?*
Doktor **mu**?	*Is she / he a doctor?*
İngiliz **miyiz**?	*Are we English?*
İspanyol **musunuz**?	*Are you Spanish?*
Türk **mü**? / (Türk **müler**?)	*Are they Turks / Turkish?*

Note: The word **miyim** in **Sekreter miyim?** is made from **mi** and **im** coming together. You need a 'buffer y' as explained earlier. Can you spot another 'buffer y' in the examples above? Yes, it is the 'buffer y' in **İngiliz miyiz?**

More about adjectives

One of the great features of the Turkish language is that a few adjectives and nouns can get you a long way, providing you learn some word endings! Here are a few more ways of extending your word power by adding some endings.

As you saw earlier in the unit, Turkish adjectives can take personal endings.

güzel *beautiful*	**güzeller** *they are beautiful*	**güzelim** *I am beautiful*

It is also possible to make adjectives from some nouns. For example, by adding -lı, -li, -lu or -lü to the name of many countries or cities, you change the word from a noun naming a place to an adjective or noun indicating a person *from* that country or city.

Kanada	*Canada*	Kanadalı	*from Canada*
İzmir	*Izmir*	İzmirli	*from Izmir*
İstanbul	*Istanbul*	İstanbullu	*from Istanbul*
Ürgüp	*Ürgüp*	Ürgüplü	*from Ürgüp*

Words indicating nationality which are formed in this way can be nouns or adjectives. So **Danimarkalı** can be translated as *Danish* (adjective) or *a Dane* (noun).

Some nationality words do not take the -lı, -li, -lu, -lü endings, for example, **Türk, İngiliz, Fransız, Alman**.

More ways of using the *lı, li, lu, lü* endings

The endings **lı, li, lu** and **lü** are added to the singular of nouns to make nouns or adjectives with the following meanings:

a Added to the name of a quality, they mean someone or something possessing that quality:

şeker	*sugar*	şekerli	*sweet*
akıl	*intelligence*	akıllı	*intelligent*
bulut	*cloud*	bulutlu	*cloudy*

b Possessing that quality to a higher degree:

sevgi	*affection*	sevgili	*beloved*
yaş	*age*	yaşlı	*aged, old*

c Added to the name of a colour, they form an adjective or noun meaning, dressed in that colour:

beyaz	*white*	beyazlı	*dressed in white*
mavi	*blue*	mavili	*dressed in blue*

d These endings may be added to a phrase to extend its meaning, so:

uzun boy	*long stature*	**uzun boylu**	*tall*
kısa saç	*short hair*	**kısa saçlı**	*short haired*
orta yaş	*middle age*	**orta yaşlı**	*middle aged*
mavi göz	*blue eyes*	**mavi gözlü**	*blue eyed*

Now that you have learnt several word endings and some of the ways in which they build meaning from root words, you might start noticing that some words have combinations of these word parts:

ev   *house*
evli   *married* (literally translated as *with house*)
evlilik   *marriage* (literally *the state of being with a house*)

As you saw earlier in the unit the ending **-li** means *with*, the ending **-lik** denotes the formation of an abstract noun. You will learn more about this later.

Word order and adjectives

Now that you know how to make more adjectives, you need to make sure you put them in the correct place in the sentence. In Turkish, adjectives come before nouns, as in English: **güzel kadın** (*beautiful woman*), **uzun saç** (*long hair*). The **bir**, which acts like the indefinite article (*a, an*), usually comes between the adjective and noun: **güzel bir kadın** (*beautiful a woman*) **yakışıklı bir erkek** (*handsome a man*).

Tag questions

Soğuk, değil mi?   *Cold, isn't it?*

Tag questions invite you to either agree or disagree, often very briefly with a 'yes' or 'no': In English, tag questions are very difficult to form, as the tag (*wasn't it? aren't they? don't they? have you? did she?* etc.) changes according to the tenses, whether the sentence is positive or negative, and the personal pronoun. The good news is that in Turkish, question tags are very straightforward: they always stay the same!

Sen akıllısın, değil mi?   *You are clever, aren't you?*
Evet, akıllıyım.   *Yes, I am.*

O akıllı değil, değil mi?   *He is not clever, is he?*
Hayır, değil. (Evet, değil.)   *No, he isn't. (Yes, he isn't.)*

In the last example, there are two ways of expressing the same answer, but both answers show agreement that he is not clever. **Evet** or **Hayır** would be the informal short answer.

ℹ️ Addressing people correctly

In Turkey, only people who are very close call each other by their first names (see Unit 1), and then only if they are more or less the same age. In the case of an age gap, the younger person will use an additional polite address form when speaking to the older person. For an older woman this would be **Hanım**, as in **Gül Hanım**, or just **Hanımefendi**. For an older man, this would be **Bey** as in **Ahmet Bey** or just **Beyefendi**. If you are addressing an older person who also has a professional title, the professional title comes first, as in **Doktor Bahadır Bey** or just **Doktor Bey**, **Profesör Hanım**, **Garson Bey**. **Hanım** is the equivalent of *Ms*, *Miss*, or *Mrs* and **Bey** is the equivalent of *Mr*. The important thing to remember, though, is that they are used with the first name, not the surname (surnames were only introduced during Atatürk's reforms).

Practice

1 Translate these sentences into English.

   a Tarkan çok yakışıklı bir erkek.
   b Sezen Aksu çok güzel bir kadın.
   c Öğretmenler çok akıllı mı?
   d Çalışkan bir öğrencisin.
   e Türkçe çok ilginç.
   f Türkiye hem tarihi hem modern bir ülke.
   g Türkiye'de çok işsiz var.
   h Türkçe çok kolay.
   i İngilizce zengin bir dil, değil mi?
   j Almanca ve Fransızca gramer zor.

2 Match the following famous people with their nationality and their native language. The first one has been done for you.

Person	Nationality	Language
a Atatürk ———	A Türk ———	i Türkçe
b Napoleon	B Alman	ii Fransızca
c Hemingway	C İspanyol	iii İspanyolca
d Shakespeare	D Rus	iv Almanca
e Goya	E Fransız	v Rusça
f M. Gandhi	F Amerikalı	vi İngilizce
g Tchaikovsky	G İngiliz	vii Hintçe
h Bach	H Hintli	viii İngilizce

3 Match the sentences (a–i) with the pictures (1–9).

a Çok güzel bir film, değil mi?
b Siz, Timur'sunuz, değil mi? Ben, Ahmet.
c Yiyecekler çok lezzetli, değil mi?
d Bu program çok ilginç değil, değil mi?
e Bebek çok güzel, değil mi?
f Doğru değil, değil mi?
g Burası biraz soğuk, değil mi?
h Çiçekler çok güzel, değil mi?
i Tarkan iyi bir şarkıcı, değil mi?

▶ 4 Andy and Ayşegül are having a party at their house in Birmingham. The guests mingle and chat to each other. Choose an answer from the box below to complete the following conversations, then check your answers on the recording. (They're also given in the Key at the back of the book.)

a Ben İstanbul'luyum.
   İstanbul'un neresinden?
   ....

b Bu tatilde Türkiye'deyiz.
   Türkiye'nin neresinde?
   ....

c Bu Türkçe'de ne demek?   d Bu İngilizce'de ne demek?

....

e Siz manken misiniz?   f Ben 45 yaşındayım.
   Hayır, sekreterim. Ya siz?   ....

....

g Bu telefon numaram   h Ben İngilizim.
   595 33 22.   Gerçekten mi?
   Bu da benim telefon   ....
   numaram 454 78 81.

....

i Ben bekarım. Ya, siz?   j Tarkan Alman mı?

....

*neresinde? *whereabouts?*

i	Ben evliyim. Eşim orada.	vi	Harita demek.
ii	Evet, Londra'lıyım.	vii	Ben 23 yaşındayım.
iii	Ben öğrenciyim.	viii	Map demek.
iv	Hayır, Türk.	ix	Güneyde, Alanya'da.
v	Teşekkürler.	x	Ataköy.

5 Match the questions in the left-hand column with their corresponding answer from the right-hand column.

a Ankara nerede?   i Türkiye'de.
b Paris nerede?   ii Brüksel Belçika'da.
c Londra İngiltere'de mi?   iii Paris Fransa'da.
d New York nerede?   iv Evet, Japonya'da.
e Barselona İtalya'da mı?   v Evet, İngiltere'de.
f Roma nerede?   vi New York Amerika'da.
g Moskova Rusya'da,   vii Hayır, Barselona
   değil mi?   İspanya'da.
h Samsun nerede?   viii Roma İtalya'da.
i Tokyo Japonya'da, değil mi?   ix Evet, Rusya'da.
j Brüksel nerede?   x Samsun, kuzey
   Türkiye'de.

▶ 6 Listen to the recording, then complete the following table. The first line has been done for you.

Name	Nationality	Job	Marital status	Age	Home town
Bülent	Turkish	doctor	__	__	Izmir
Lucy					
Trish Webb					
Phillipe					
Ülkü Gezer					
June					

▶ 7 **Pronunciation: ö, p, r.** Listen to the following sounds on the recording and copy until you are confident with your pronunciation.

ö	p	r
öç	ip	ar
ön	pil	er
çöp	çap	re
yön	pat	kar

▶ Mini-test

Well done; you have now completed Unit 7! Give yourself a point for each of the following questions that you answer correctly in Turkish without looking at the book.

1 Ask someone if they are from America (if they are American).
2 Ask someone how old they are.
3 Ask someone what nationality they are.
4 Say you are married.
5 Ask someone if they are single.
6 What are the appropriate ways of addressing someone older than you and someone younger than you?

Points:_____/6

8

shopping

In this unit you will learn
- how to shop for presents
- how to say what is happening
- how to talk about your daily routine
- how to talk about what will happen shortly
- pronunciation: s, ş, t

▶ Dialogue 1 Planning the day

Listen to the recording several times before answering the following questions.

Questions

1 What do they want to do today?
2 Where are they going to go?

Laura and Ben are talking about what they are going to do.

Ben	Bugün ne yapıyoruz?
Laura	Bilmiyorum. Ben hediye almak istiyorum.
Ben	Ben de deri ceket, ayakkabı ve lokum almak istiyorum.
Laura	Kapalı Çarşı'ya gidelim mi? (*Laura looks at her shopping list.*) Bluz, çanta, baharat, ayakkabı ve hediyelik şeyler.
Ben	Nereye gidelim?
Laura	Ben Kapalı Çarşı'ya ve Taksim'e gitmek istiyorum.
Ben	Tamam, gidelim.

bugün	*today*
yapmak	*to do*
hediye	*present*
almak	*to buy*
istemek	*to want*
deri	*leather*
ceket	*jacket*
ayakkabı	*shoes*
Kapalı Çarşı	*Grand Bazaar*
bluz	*blouse*
çanta	*bag*
baharat	*spices*
hediyelik şeyler	*presents*
nereye gidelim?	*where shall we go?*

ℹ️ Shopping in Turkey is an experience in itself, whether you are bargaining for a kilim in the bustling **Kapalı Çarşı** *Grand Bazaar* in Istanbul, choosing clothes in a smart boutique or buying local produce in a country market. Don't be surprised if you are offered a glass of tea as you view a range of carpets or leather jackets!

Many big towns and cities have permanent covered markets and spice markets. In Istanbul, the historic **Kapalı Çarşı** is an indoor maze of over 4,000 shops, selling carpets, antiques, jewellery, leather goods, clothing and textiles. Its vaulted stone passages also house banks, restaurants, Turkish baths, cafés and mosques.

The **Mısır Çarşısı** *Egyptian Bazaar* gets its name from the ancient tradition of trade with Egypt in coffee, rice, incense and henna. Today you can still buy coffee, spices, fruit and herb teas, nuts and dried fruit – as well as aphrodisiacs!

▶ Dialogue 2 Buying bags

Later on, in Istanbul's Grand Bazaar…

Laura	Merhaba.
Salesperson	İyi günler. Buyrun, efendim.
Laura	Deri çantalar kaç lira?
Salesperson	Büyük 15, orta 10 ve küçükler de 5 milyon lira.
Laura	Şu orta boy, lütfen. 10 milyon çok pahalı, 4 milyon olur mu?
Salesperson	Ne renk?
Laura	Siyah, lütfen.
Salesperson	Buyrun. Sizin için 5 milyon.
Laura	Tamam. (*Laura hands over the money.*)
Salesperson	Güle güle kullanın.
Laura	Teşekkür ederim.

Questions

1 Laura ne renk çanta alıyor?
2 Laura pazarlık yapıyor mu?

çanta	bag
büyük	big
orta	medium
küçük	small
orta boy	medium sized
sizin için	for you
Güle güle kullanın!	Enjoy using it!*

*This is a commonly-used pleasantry. Its literal translation is *use in happy days*. It's said to people who have bought or who have been given something new. For clothes **Güle güle giy!** *enjoy wearing it*, would be used.

► **Dialogue 3 Buying spices**

Listen to the recording several times – it will become clearer each time you listen to it.

Laura and Ben walk to the spice market to buy spices and dried fruit.

Stallholder	Buyrun?
Laura	Baharat almak istiyoruz.
Stallholder	Neler almak istiyorsunuz?
Laura	Köftelik baharat, kimyon, sumak falan.
Stallholder	Ne kadar?
Laura	Yüz gramlık paketler.
Stallholder	Başka bir şey istiyor musunuz?
Ben	Bu ne?
Stallholder	Padişah macunu.
Ben	Padişah macunu ne demek?
Stallholder	Afrodiziyak demek.
Ben	Benim için gerek yok. Ben istemiyorum. (*laughter*) Biraz kuru yemiş istiyorum.
Stallholder	Ne kadar?
Ben	Yarım kilo kayısı, yarım kilo incir. Fındık var mı? Güzel mi?

The stallholder offers them some nuts to try.

Ben	Evet! Yarım kilo karışık fıstık, lütfen. Hepsi bu kadar. Kaç lira?
Stallholder	10 milyon. Sudan ucuz!

Questions

1 Kim baharat alıyor?
2 Ben afrodiziyak istiyor mu?
3 Ben ne kadar fıstık alıyor?

baharat	spices
köftelik	for meatballs
kimyon	cumin
sumak	sumac
falan	and such like, etc.
gramlık	gram
paket	packet
başka bir şey	anything else
padişah macunu	aphrodisiacs
gerek	necessary
kuru yemiş	dried fruit
kayısı	apricot
yarım	half
incir	fig
fındık	hazelnuts
fıstık	nuts
hepsi bu kadar	that's all
sudan ucuz*	very cheap

*Sudan ucuz is an expression which means *very very cheap*. Literally it means *even cheaper than water*.

i Turkish delight is called **Lokum** in Turkish. It was invented by Ali Muhiddin Hacı Bekir in the 16th century. He came up with a translucent jelly-like sweet made from a mixture of refined sugar, lemon juice and cornflour, which tastes heavenly. The new sweet came to the attention of Sultan Abdulhamid and he liked it so much that Hacı Bekir became confectioner to the court. The story goes that the name 'Turkish delight' was coined when an English traveller took some **Lokum** home to a friend who was 'delighted' by it!

Hacı Bekir's shop was established in 1777 and is still run by his family. It can be found at 81–3 Hamidiye Caddesi, the street which runs between Istanbul's main railway station and The Egyptian Bazaar. Here you will find all kinds of **Lokum** and various sweets stored in big jars and laid out on trays. You will also find a more modern shop in Taksim, in Istanbul.

Lokum comes in various flavours: rosewater, fruit or peppermint, and it is sometimes filled with pistachios, hazelnuts or ground apricots. **Lokum** remains popular among Turks and tourists alike. It tends to be eaten on special occasions, holidays and birthdays. It also makes an ideal gift if you are invited to someone's house. There is an old Turkish saying, **tatlı yiyelim, tatlı konuşalım** *eat sweetly and you shall speak sweetly.*

▶ Dialogue 4 Buying Turkish delight

Listen to the recording and answer the following questions.

Having bought their spices, Laura and Ben want to buy Turkish delight from the famous Hacı Bekir Turkish delight and sweet shop.

Questions

1 Do Laura and Ben haggle?
2 Do they get the recipe for Turkish delight?

Laura	Afedersiniz, Hacı Bekir Lokumcusu, nerede?
Stallholder	Düz gidin, sağa dönün solda.
Laura	Teşekkürler.
Stallholder	Rica ederim.

They go into the Hacı Bekir sweet shop.

Shop assistant	Buyrun, efendim.
Laura	Lokum almak istiyoruz, kaç lira?
Shop assistant	Hangi çeşit?
Ben	Neler var?

The assistant holds out a tray of free samples, pointing out the different types.

| Shop assistant | Bu naneli, bu gül, bu sade, bu da fıstıklı. Buyrun. Tatlı yiyelim, tatlı konuşalım. Tatlı yerken biz her zaman böyle diyoruz. |
| Laura and Ben | Mmmm. |

Laura and Ben both love the Turkish delight and they decide to buy some of their presents from here.

| Shop assistant | Yarım kilo karışık – 3 milyon lira. |
| Laura | Yarım kiloluk dört kutu karışık, lütfen. |

While their Turkish delight is being put into special boxes, wrapped and sealed, Ben asks some questions.

| Ben | Dükkan yeni mi? |
| Shop assistant | Hayır, biz 1777'den beri lokum yapıyoruz. Lokumlarımız çok taze. Her gün yeni lokum geliyor. Bugün tüm dünyaya satıyoruz. Her hafta değişik bir çeşit yapıyoruz. |

Ben   Nasıl yapıyorsunuz?
Shop assistant Şeker, fıstık ve ... koyuyoruz ama tarifi bizim sırrımız.
Ben   Lokumu daha çok turistlere mi satıyorsunuz?
Shop assistant Hayır, biz Türkler özel günlerde ve ziyaretlerde birbirimize hep hediye olarak lokum veriyoruz.

lokumcu	*Turkish delight shop*
rica ederim	*not at all*
lokum	*Turkish delight*
çeşit	*kind, type*
naneli	*peppermint-flavoured*
gül	*rose-flavoured*
sade	*plain*
fıstıklı	*nutty*
Tatlı yiyelim, tatlı konuşalım	*Let's eat sweet, speak sweet.* (a common saying when offering sweets)
yerken	*while eating*
her zaman	*always*
kiloluk	*for a kilo*
kutu	*box*
1777'den beri	*since 1777*
taze	*fresh*
her	*every*
tüm	*all*
dünya	*world*
satmak	*to sell*
değişik	*different*
koymak	*to put*
tarif	*recipe*
sırrımız	*our secret*
turist	*tourist*
özel	*special*
ziyaret	*visit*
birbirimiz	*each other*
hep	*all*
olarak	*as*
vermek	*to give*

Questions
3 Kaç kutu lokum alıyorlar?
4 Dükkan yeni mi?
5 Lokumlar çok taze, değil mi?

▶ Dialogue 5 Buying clothes

Later that afternoon, Laura goes to a clothes shop to buy a blouse.

Shop assistant	Buyrun, efendim.
Laura	Bir bluz bakıyorum.
Shop assistant	Kaç beden?
Laura	38.
Shop assistant	Buyrun. Bu bluz çok güzel.
Laura	Yeşil bana yakışmıyor. Mavi veya beyaz var mı?
Shop assistant	Buyrun. Bir mavi, bir beyaz, 38 beden.
Laura	Kaç lira?
Shop assistant	58 milyon.
Laura	Denemek istiyorum.
Shop assistant	Tabii.

Laura tries on the blouse.

Laura	Bunu alıyorum. Kaç lira?
Shop assistant	58 milyon.
Laura	Çok pahalı. 40 milyon veriyorum.
Shop assistant	Burada pazarlık yapmıyoruz. Sizin için 50 milyon lira.
Laura	Tamam, alıyorum.

Questions

1 Laura kaç giyiyor?
2 Yeşil Laura'ya yakışmıyor mu?

bluz	*blouse*
bakmak	*to look*
kaç beden?	*what size?*
yakışmak	*to suit*
denemek	*to try on*
pazarlık	*bargain*
pazarlık yapmak	*to bargain, haggle*
sizin için	*for you*

i Turkish sizes for clothing and shoes are the same as European sizes.

Women's clothes								Men's clothes				
British	10	12	14	16	18	20	22	British	37–8	39–40	41–2	43–4
European	38	40	42	44	46	48	50	European	94–7	99–102	104–107	109–112
American	8	10	12	14	16	18	20	American	38	40	42	44

Women's shoes								Men's shoes							
British	3	4	5	6	7	8	9	British	7	8	9	10	11	12	13
European	35	36	38	39	40	42	43	European	41	42	43	44	45	46	47
American	4	5	6	7	8	9	10	American	8	9	10	11	12	13	14

Language points

Using the *-iyor* present tense

In the dialogues, you will notice that we have introduced a new tense, the **-iyor** present tense. For example, in Dialogue 5 above, Laura says, '**Bunu alıyorum**' '*I'll take it*'. This literally means '*I'm taking it.*'

The **-iyor** tense has several purposes. These are shown in the table below.

Purpose	Example	Translation
Describing something happening now	Alışveriş yapıyoruz.	*We're shopping.*
Stating an unchanging fact	Alkol kullanmıyorum.	*I don't drink alcohol.*
Describing a habitual repeated action	Türkler sık sık çay içiyorlar.	*Turks often drink tea.*
Describing something that will happen soon	Bugün alışveriş yapıyoruz.	*We're shopping today.*
Stating how long you have been doing something	1777'den beri lokum yapıyoruz / satıyoruz.	*We've been making / selling Turkish delight since 1777.*

The **-iyor** present tense is also used to express senses and emotions which in English are expressed in the simple present tense: **Biliyorum.** *I know.* (lit. *I'm knowing.*) **Seviyorum.** *I love.* (lit. *I'm loving.*) **Görüyorum.** *I see/I can see.* (lit. *I'm seeing.*) **İşitiyorum.** *I hear/I can hear.* (lit. *I'm hearing.*) **Hissediyorum.** *I feel.* (lit. *I'm feeling.*)

To use this tense, you need to remember to add two verb endings: the tense ending and the correct personal ending.

For the present -iyor tense, the endings are:

1 for the tense:

-ıyor, -iyor, -uyor, -üyor (according to the rules of vowel harmony), or simply -yor after a verb ending in a vowel. If the verb stem ends in **a** or **e** then these vowels are replaced by ı and i respectively.

2 personal endings:

-um	*I*	-uz	*we*
-sun	*You*	-sunuz	*you*
(none)	*He / she / it*	-ler / lar	*they*

For example, *to buy / take / get / receive* is **almak**.

Stem	Tense ending	Personal ending
al-	-ıyor	-um

I am buying. **Alıyorum.**

The verb *want / would like* is **istemek**; the stem is **iste-** but the **e** changes to **i**:

Stem	Tense ending	Personal ending
isti-	-yor	-um

I want / would like **istiyorum ...**

Some sample verbs:

	istemek *to want / would like*	ödemek *to pay*	almak *to buy / take / get / receive*
I	istiyorum	ödüyorum	alıyorum
you	istiyorsun	ödüyorsun	alıyorsun
he / she / it	istiyor	ödüyor	alıyor
we	istiyoruz	ödüyoruz	alıyoruz
you	istiyorsunuz	ödüyorsunuz	alıyorsunuz
they	istiyorlar	ödüyorlar	alıyorlar

Negatives

If you want to make a verb negative in the -iyor present tense, you add -m to the stem before the -iyor / -yor ending:

Onu almıyorum.	*I am not buying that.*
Pazarlık etmiyorum.	*I am not haggling.*
Şapka giymiyorum.	*I am not wearing a hat.*
Anlamıyorum.	*I don't understand.*

Questions

If you want to turn a statement into a question in the –iyor present tense, you add mı-, mi-, mu- or mü- before the personal ending. In the written form, the two parts of the verb are separate, though they are spoken as one word:

Alıyor **musun?**	*Are you buying?*
Deniyor **musun?**	*Are you trying it on?*
Deri seviyor **musunuz?**	*Do you like leather?*
Kredi kartı alıyor **musunuz?**	*Do you take credit cards?*

Note: When you make questions using question words such as **Ne?** *What?*, **Kaç?** *How much / many?*, **Kim?** *Who?*, **Nasıl?** *How is it? / What is it like?*, **Nerede?** *Where?*, **Neden?** *Why?*, **Niçin?** *Why?*, etc. you don't use **mu-** or its variations – you use the question word instead.

Ne istiyorsunuz?	*What would you like?*
Kaç tane istiyorsunuz?	*How many do you want?*

Pairs

In English, some items of clothing are usually spoken of as being in a pair, such as a pair of shoes, socks, gloves or slippers. You can choose to translate this expression literally in Turkish: **Bir çift ayakkabı almak istiyorum.** *I'd like to buy a pair of shoes.* But if you say **Ayakkabı almak istiyorum** (*I'd like to buy shoes*) your listener will normally assume that you want a pair of shoes.

However, English also talks of pairs of trousers, spectacles, glasses and tights, referring to only one item! In these instances, you would never say **bir çift** in Turkish, you would always refer to **bir pantalon, külotlu çorap, gözlük**. If you asked for 'pantolonlar' in Turkey, the shopkeeper would think you wanted more than one pair!

bir pantalon	*a pair of trousers*
bir çift ayakkabı	*a pair of shoes*
bir gözlük	*a pair of glasses*
eldiven	*a pair of gloves.*
Pantalon almak istiyorum.	*I'd like to buy a pair of trousers.*
(Bir çift) ayakkabı almak istiyorum.	*I'd like to buy a pair of shoes.*

Practice

▶1 Picture dictation. Read or listen to the Turkish passage below, draw the scene on a piece of paper and then check it with the answer at the back of the book.

Suzan deniz kenarında bir kafede oturuyor. Meyve suyu içerken plajda ve denizdeki insanlara bakıyor. Üç çocuk dondurma alıyor. Bir çift kumlarda yatıyor. Bikinili ve şapkalı kadın kitap okuyor. Şortlu ve gözlüklü erkek denize bakıyor. Denizde bir sandal ve bir yelkenli var. Yedi kişi yüzüyor.

oturuyor	*sitting* (**oturmak** *to sit*)
plaj	*beach*
insanlar	*people*
çift	*couple*
yatıyor	*lying* (**yatmak** *to lie down*)
okuyor	*reading* (**okumak** *to read*)
kitap	*book*
şort	*shorts*
sandal	*rowing boat*
yelkenli	*sailing boat*
kişi	*person*
yüzüyor	*swimming* (**yüzmek** *to swim*)

▶ 2 A woman is in a clothes shop talking to the salesperson. Unscramble the following dialogue, and check it at the back of the book, or by listening to the recording.

a Kaç beden?

b 40.

c Kaç lira?

d 80 milyon.

e Buyrun, efendim.

f Buyrun, bu pantalon çok güzel.

g Bir pantalon bakıyorum.

h Buyrun bir siyah, bir gri. 40 beden.

i Kahverengi bana yakışmıyor. Siyah veya gri var mı?

j Tabii.

k Denemek istiyorum, lütfen.

3 Here are some items that you may like to buy in Turkey. Sort them into groups under the headings supplied:

Food	Clothes	Presents

çerez kilim elma çay lokum

fıstık T-shirt

padişah macunu CD bluz

incir pantalon ceket

kaset çanta Türk kahvesi halı

ayakkabı bal cüzdan baharat

elma çay	apple tea
kaset	tape
halı	carpet
cüzdan	wallet, purse

4 Wordsearch. Find ten items you can buy in Turkey.

A	G	L	O	K	U	M	K	D	N
B	S	T	O	B	P	H	R	E	F
A	Y	A	K	K	A	B	I	R	I
H	U	B	S	İ	T	Ş	Z	İ	S
A	V	L	M	L	R	A	E	G	T
R	T	U	E	İ	K	P	O	H	I
A	R	Z	P	M	T	K	H	E	K
T	O	P	A	N	T	A	L	O	N
I	E	T	R	B	R	P	A	Y	T
C	E	K	E	T	P	U	G	U	Z

5 **Pronunciation: s, ş, t.** Listen several times and repeat until you are confident with your pronunciation.

s	ş	t
as	aş	at
es	eş	et
su	iş	ot
sis	şu	tüy

▶ Mini-test

You have now completed Unit 8. Now you will be able to shop for presents and to haggle. You will also be able to talk about your daily routine and what will happen shortly. Give yourself a point for each of the following things you can say in Turkish without looking at the book.

1 Ask for a blue jacket in size 40.
2 Ask for some peppermint-flavoured Turkish delight.
3 Ask for half a kilo of dried fruit.
4 Buy a packet of cumin.
5 Say 'I don't drink wine' in Turkish.
6 Ask for a pair of shoes, size 41.
7 Ask for a pair of blue trousers.

Points:_____/7

09 where shall we go?

In this unit you will learn
- how to make arrangements to go out or suggest doing something
- how to tell the time
- how to book a seat at the theatre
- how to buy tickets for public transport
- how to make, accept or refuse an invitation
- pronunciation: u, ü, v

▶ Dialogue 1 What shall we do at the weekend?

Listen to the dialogue a few times before answering Questions 1 and 2. Listen to the dialogue again, read it, then answer Questions 3–7.

Questions

1 What are Şafak and Banu going to do at the weekend?
2 How do they find out what's on?

Banu and Şafak are talking about what to do at the weekend.

Şafak Hafta sonunda ne yapalım?
Banu Tiyatro'ya gidelim mi? Kenterler'de çok güzel bir oyun var.
Şafak Ne oynuyor?
Banu Bakalım. Galiba *Hep aşk vardı* oynuyor.
They look at the Kenter theatre's schedule.
Şafak *Hep aşk vardı* oynuyor, saat 8.30'da.
Banu Evet, harika. Ben *Hamam'*ı da görmek istiyorum ama.
Şafak *Hamam'*ı ben de görmek istiyorum.
Banu Önce Kenterler'i arayayım mı?
Şafak Hadi, arayalım.
The telephone rings, but there is no reply.
Şafak Saat kaç?
Banu Yarım. Öğle tatili.
Şafak Bir buçukta tekrar arayalım.
Banu Tamam.

Questions

3 Sinemaya mı, tiyatroya mı gitmek istiyorlar?
4 Hangi tiyatroya gidiyorlar?
5 *Hamam* film mi, oyun mu?
6 Saat kaçta tiyatroya telefon ediyorlar?
7 Bu hafta sonu siz ne yapıyorsunuz?

hafta	*week*
hafta sonu	*weekend*
ne yapalım?	*what shall we do?*
tiyatro	*theatre*
gidelim mi?	*shall we go?*
ne oynuyor?	*what's on?*
bakalım	*let's have a look*
galiba	*I think, perhaps, maybe*

Hep aşk vardı	*There has always been Love* (the name of a play)
Hamam	*Turkish Bath* (the name of a Turkish film)
görmek	*to see*
istiyorum	*I want / I would like*
aramak	*to call*
arayayım	*let me call* (I'll call)
hadi, arayalım	*let's call*
yarım	*half past twelve*
bir buçukta	*at half past one*
tamam	*OK*

ⓘ Kenterler

Müşfik and Yıldız Kenter are brother and sister. They established the first really successful private theatre company in modern Turkey, which is still famous for high-quality productions.

ⓘ Hamam

The cinema is a very popular form of entertainment in Turkey. *Hamam The Turkish Bath* was released in 1997. It tells the story of an Italian who inherited a Turkish bath and leaves Italy to go and run it.

If you have the opportunity, it's worth watching a Turkish film as it will give you a greater insight into Turkish culture. If the film is subtitled you will also be able to hear Turkish being spoken and perhaps you'll be able to understand some of it.

Language points

Telling the time

There are two ways of telling the time in Turkish, first the 24-hour clock and second the 12-hour clock. The international 24-hour clock is very simple; all you need to do is revise the numbers you have already learnt! The 24-hour clock is used at airports and stations, and also on the radio and television. However, for everyday purposes most Turkish people use the 12-hour clock and you will need to learn a few more words. When you are talking about the time in Turkish there is no distinction between a.m. or p.m. Usually, people will be able to tell if you are talking about morning, afternoon or evening by the context of the conversation. But just to make sure, you can add the Turkish for morning and say **sabah sekizde** *at eight in* *the morning*, **öğleden sonra üçte** *at three in the afternoon*, **akşam altıda** *at six in the evening*, **gece onda** *at ten at night*.

Here is some useful vocabulary about time:

saat	*time, hour or clock*
saat kaç?	*what time is it?*
saat kaçta?	*at what time?*
kaç saat?	*how many hours?*
dakika	*minutes*
saniye	*seconds*
çeyrek	*a quarter*
buçuk	*it's half past*
buçukta	*at half past*
geçiyor (-ı, -i, -u, -ü)	*past*
var (-e, -a)	*to*
öğlen	*midday*
gece yarısı	*midnight*

▶ Saat kaç? *What time is it?*

The 24-hour clock

a	b	c	d	e
12:00	12:10	12:15	12:30	12:40
oniki	oniki on	oniki onbeş	oniki otuz (yarım)	oniki kırk

f	g	h	i	j
14:00	18:10	19:20	20:35	21:45
ondört	onsekiz on	ondokuz yirmi	yirmi otuzbeş	yirmibir kırkbeş

The 12-hour clock

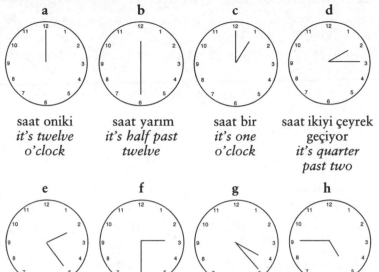

a
saat oniki
*it's twelve
o'clock*

b
saat yarım
*it's half past
twelve*

c
saat bir
*it's one
o'clock*

d
saat ikiyi çeyrek
geçiyor
*it's quarter
past two*

e
saat ikiyi yirmi
beş geçiyor
*it's twenty-five
past two*

f
saat
üç buçuk
*it's half
pas two*

g
saat dördü
yirmi beş geçiyor
*it's twenty-five
past four*

h
saat beşe
çeyrek var
*it's quarter
to five*

Saat *Time, hour, clock*

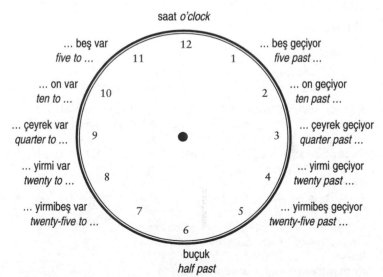

saat *o'clock*

... beş var
five to ...

... beş geçiyor
five past ...

... on var
ten to ...

... on geçiyor
ten past ...

... çeyrek var
quarter to ...

... çeyrek geçiyor
quarter past ...

... yirmi var
twenty to ...

... yirmi geçiyor
twenty past ...

... yirmibeş var
twenty-five to ...

... yirmibeş geçiyor
twenty-five past ...

buçuk
half past

▶ The effect of vowel harmony

Look at clock **d**: why **ikiyi çeyrek geçiyor**, why not just **iki çeyrek geçiyor?**.

Look at clock **h**: why **beşe çeyrek var**, why not simply **beş çeyrek var?**

Geçiyor gives the hour -ı (-i, -u, -ü) endings according to vowel harmony.

biri beş geçiyor *five past one*	yediyi beş geçiyor
ikiyi beş geçiyor	sekizi beş geçiyor
üçü beş geçiyor	dokuzu beş geçiyor
dördü beş geçiyor	onu beş geçiyor
beşi beş geçiyor	onbiri beş geçiyor
altıyı beş geçiyor	onikiyi beş geçiyor

Var gives the hour the ending **-e** (**-a**) according to vowel harmony.

bire beş var *five to one*	yediye beş var
ikiye beş var	sekize beş var
üçe beş var	dokuza beş var
dörde beş var	ona beş var
beşe beş var	onbire beş var
altıya beş var	onikiye beş var

▶ Dialogue 2 Booking seats at the theatre

Questions

1 Are there any seats available for this Sunday?
2 How many tickets do they want to reserve?

Receptionist	Buyrun. 0212 246 35 89, Kenter Tiyatrosu.
Şafak	İyi günler. Bu pazar *Hep aşk vardı* için iki bilet ayırtmak istiyoruz.
Receptionist	İyi günler, efendim. Maalesef bu pazar için hiç bilet yok ama gelecek pazar için yer var.
Şafak	Fiyatlar nasıl acaba?
Receptionist	Tam 15 milyon lira, öğrenci, 5 milyon lira, öğretmen ve emekli 12 milyon lira.
Şafak	İki bilet, bir tam ve bir öğrenci, lütfen.
Receptionist	Nasıl ödüyorsunuz? Kartla mı?
Şafak	Evet.
Receptionist	Kart numaranız, lütfen?
Şafak	1234 1234 1234 1234.

Questions

Are Statements 3–6 true (**doğru**) or false (**yanlış**)?

3 Kenter sinemasına gidiyorlar.
4 Bu pazar için bilet yok.
5 Öğrenci daha pahalı.
6 Kredi kartı ile ödüyorlar.
7 Siz tiyatro seviyor musunuz?

buyrun	On the phone it means: *Yes, I'm listening to you! How can I help you?*
ayırtmak	*to book, to reserve*
maalesef	*unfortunately*
gelecek	*next, coming*
yer	*place, seat*
fiyatlar	*prices*
nasıl	*how*
tam	*adult/full price*
öğrenci	*student*
emekli	*retired*
ödemek	*to pay*
kartla	*by card*
kart / kredi kartı	*card / credit card*

▶ Dialogue 3 Choosing a film to watch

Questions

1 Where are Banu and Şafak going?
2 Are they going by car?

Şafak Bu akşam sinemaya gidiyor muyuz?
Banu Hadi. *Hamam'*ı görelim.
Şafak Bakalım sinemalarda hangi filmler var.
Banu ABC'de *Vampirler* var.
Şafak Ben korku filmi görmek istemiyorum.
Banu Hisar'da *Şaban* oynuyor.
Şafak O komedi değil mi?
Banu Evet, ama ben *Hamam'*ı görmek istiyorum.
Şafak Saat kaçta?
Banu looks at the newspaper.
Banu Beşte, yedide ve dokuzda.
Şafak Yediye gidelim mi?

Banu	Tamam. Hadi şimdi çıkalım.
Şafak	Araba bozuk. Dolmuşla mı, otobüsle mi gidiyoruz? Otobüs daha ucuz, dolmuş daha rahat.
Banu	Fark etmez.
Şafak	Hadi otobüsle gidelim.

Questions

3 Sinemalarda hangi filmler var?
4 Hangi filme gidiyorlar?
5 Saat kaçta?
6 Neyle gidiyorlar?
7 Niçin otobüsle gidiyorlar?
8 Siz hangi tür filmleri seviyorsunuz?

akşam	*evening*
hadi	*let's / come on*
korku	*horror*
komedi	*comedy*
dolmuşla	*by dolmuş* (shared taxi)
otobüsle	*by bus*
rahat	*comfortable*

i Dolmuş

In some towns shared taxis called **dolmuş** operate on certain routes. **Dolmuş** only go when they are full (**dolmuş** means literally *it is filled up*). You can get on and off the **dolmuş** at any point along its route. **Dolmuş** are cheaper than ordinary taxis. The price is in proportion to the distance you travel. You can recognize a **dolmuş** by the sign on the roof or windscreen.

▶ Dialogue 4 Buying bus tickets

Şafak and Banu go to the nearest bus stop to buy tickets for the bus. In Istanbul you need to buy your bus ticket before you get on a bus. This may differ from city to city or from town to town.

Questions

1 Where are Banu and Şafak going to?
2 Do they buy single or return tickets?

Şafak   Taksim'e iki bilet.
Banu   Dönüş için de al.
At the ticket office.
Şafak   Dört bilet, lütfen.
Clerk   Dört milyon lira.
Şafak hands over a 10 million lira note.
Şafak   Buyrun.
Clerk   Bozuk yok mu?
Şafak   Yok.
Clerk   (*handing over the change*) Buyrun. Altı milyon lira.

Questions

3 Otobüsle mi gidiyorlar?
4 Dönüş bileti alıyorlar mı?
5 Kart ile mi ödüyorlar?

Taksim	*Taksim Square in Istanbul*
dönüş	*return*
bozuk	*change*

Language points

İle *with/by/by means of transport*

The word **ile** means *with / by / by means of transport*.

Kartla	*with a card / by card*
Neyle (ne+ile) gidiyorsun?	*How are you getting there?* (Lit. *What are you going with / by?*)

Otobüs ile gidiyorum. Otobüs<u>le</u> gidiyorum. }	*I'm going by* (lit. *with*) *bus.*
Vapur ile gidiyorum. Vapur<u>la</u> gidiyorum. }	*I'm going by boat.*

When **ile** is shortened to an ending, it becomes **-le** or **-la** and follows the rules to vowel harmony, in the same way as the **-ler** and **-lar** endings explained in Unit 2.

Common forms of transport and where they stop

Otobüs *Bus*	Otobüs durağı *Bus stop*
Tren *Train*	İstasyon *Station*
Uçak *Aeroplane*	Havaalanı *Airport*
Vapur *Ferry*	İskele *Port*
Dolmuş *'Shared' taxi*	Dolmuş durağı *Dolmuş stop*
Taksi *Taxi*	Taksi durağı *Taxi rank*

Making suggestions, offering help, accepting or refusing an offer

As explained earlier, Turkish adds endings to verb stems to change meanings: here are some endings which show that someone is making a suggestion, offering help, or expressing a hope. Not all of the examples have an exact translation in English, so in some places we have tried to explain the sense, as well as giving a literal translation. See if you can hear your Turkish friends use these expressions. Gradually you will become more familiar with these expressions and will feel confident enough to use them.

The *let* forms of verbs

Look at the following examples, meaning *let* ...:

Yapayım (*I*)	*let me do / make* or *here I'll do / make, I'd better do it*
Yapalım (*we*)	*let's do / make, we'd better do it*
Yapsın (*his / her*)	*let her / him do* or *she / he should do, he / she'd better do*
Yapsınlar (*they*)	*let them do / make* or *they should do / make, they'd better do*

Suggestions or positive offers of help with -eyim

Add -**eyim** onto the stem of a verb to give the meaning, *let me* ... You use it to offer help or make a suggestion. For example:

Tiyatroyu arayayım.	*Let me call the theatre. / I'll call the theatre.*
Yardım edeyim.	*Let me help. / I'll help.*

Suggestions or offers of help as questions with *-eyim*

Sinemayı aray<u>ayım mı</u>?	*Shall I call the cinema?*
Yardım ed<u>eyim mi</u>?	*Shall I help?*

Negative suggestions or offer of help with *-eyim (-meyeyim)*

Şimdi ara<u>mayayım</u>.	*I don't want to call now.* (lit. *Let me not call now.*)
Tiyatroyu ara<u>mayayım</u>.	*I don't want to call the theatre.* (lit. *Let me not call the theatre.*)
Sinemayı ara<u>mayayım</u> mı?	*Don't you want me to call the cinema?* (lit. *Shouldn't I call the cinema?*)

Positive suggestions with *-elim (-elim mi)*

Add **-elim** onto the stem of a verb to give the meaning *let's*. You use it for making suggestions. It behaves in the same way as **-eyim**. For example:

Bak<u>alım</u>.	*Let's have a look. / Go on then.*
Gid<u>elim</u>.	*Let's go.*

Suggestions in question form with *-elim*

Bak<u>alım mı</u>?	*Shall we have a look?*
Gid<u>elim mi</u>?	*Shall we go?*

Suggestions as negative form with *-elim (-meyelim)*

Bak<u>mayalım</u>.	*Let's not look.*
Git<u>meyelim</u>.	*Let's not go.*
Bak<u>mayalım</u> mı?	*Shall we not have a look?*

Positive remarks with *-sin*

Add **-sin** (**-sın**, **-sun** or **sün**, according to vowel harmony) to the verb stem to say what someone should do. You can also use it to express a hope that something will happen. It is frequently used in stock phrases, as illustrated on the next page. Turkish has many of these, and for a wider range of purposes than in English. Note that the third person singular (*he, she, it*) and plural (*them*) are not very common.

Turkish	Literal translation	Meaning
Geçmiş olsun.	*Let it pass.*	*Get well soon.*
Yeni Yılın kutlu olsun.	*Let your New Year be happy.*	*Happy New Year.*
Doğum günün kutlu olsun.	*Let your birthday be happy.*	*Happy birthday.*
Üstü kalsın.	*Let the change stay.*	*Keep the change.*
Afiyet olsun.	*Let good health be.*	*Enjoy your meal.*
Bayramınız kutlu olsun.	*Let your Bayram be happy.*	*Happy holiday.*
Allah mesut etsin.	*May God give them / you happiness.*	*Said to a newly married couple.*
Kolay gelsin.	*May your work be easy.*	*Said to someone working very hard.*

i **Şeker Bakram** and **Kurban Bayramı** are both festive times when children are given new clothes, the poor are helped and family members are visited. It is usual to phone family or friends or send them **Bayram** cards.

> **Bayram**   *festivity, religious festival, national holiday, festival*

İyi Bayramlar.   *Bayramınız kutlu olsun.*

Questions with *-sin (-sin mi)*

Üstü kal<u>sın</u> mı?   *Shall I / should I leave the change?*

Negative remarks with *-sin (-masin)*

Yap<u>masın</u>.   *Don't make him or her.*
(lit. *Let him / her not do.*)

Although these forms are widely used in Turkish, in English they would be expressed very differently. So listen to your Turkish friends carefully. Try to get the gist of what is being said and try to get used to the Turkish way of thinking! All languages and all cultures have their differences. Just try to enjoy the differences!

The 'buffer y' and consonant change

If there are two vowels next to each other you insert a connecting y to make it easier to say, e.g. bakmayalım, yardım edeyim. (For a fuller explanation see Unit 5.) In addition to the 'buffer y' there are also some consonant changes in Turkish if a word finishes with a hard consonant. The hard consonants are: ç, f, h, k, p, s, ş and t.

When a hard consonant is followed by an ending which usually starts with a d you must change the d to a t. This is similar to vowel harmony, but with consonants. At this stage do not worry about getting all these changes right. It is enough for you to recognize them. Even educated native speakers sometimes make mistakes.

> Saat kaçda? *becomes* Saat kaçta? *At what time?*
> Saat ikiye *becomes* Saat ikide. *At two o'clock*

But
> Saat üçte.   *At three o'clock.*

(For more information and exercises on consonant changes see *Teach Yourself Turkish*, Unit 3.)

Practice

▶ 1 Here is a list of leisure activities (shopping, cinema, theatre, museums, restaurant, etc.). First check their meanings in the vocabulary list.

i	alışveriş yapmak	ii	sinemaya gitmek
iii	tiyatroya gitmek	iv	restorana gitmek
v	müzeye gitmek	vi	televizyon seyretmek
vii	müzik dinlemek	viii	yüzmek
ix	seyahat etmek		

a Listen to the conversation between Yeşim and Ahmet in which they discuss their plans for the evening, and list the activities you hear mentioned.
b What did they decide to do?
c Listen again and write down the dialogue.

rejimdeyim	*I am on a diet*
iyi fikir	*good idea*

▶2 Nesrin has a full week ahead of her. She goes through her diary and says what she has to do. Listen to the recording several times. Does she have any free days?

Ağustos	
4 Pazartesi	**8 Cuma**
8'de tiyatro Banu ile	*Boğaz Gezisi Yeşim ve Ahmet ile*
5 Salı	**9 Cumartesi**
	2'de Çemberlitaş Hamamı
6 Çarşamba	**10 Pazar**
1.30'da öğle yemeği Gonca ile	*Vanessa ile Karagöz ve Hacivat.*
7 Perşembe	

Now look at your diary and write out next week's entries in Turkish.

🛈 Karagöz ve Hacivat: puppets

Karagöz, a form of shadow puppet theatre, was introduced to the Ottoman Empire during the reign of Yavuz Sultan Selim in 1517. **Karagöz** and **Hacivat** are two main characters of the show.

3 Look at the following notes. Match up the invitations and replies.

a

Suzan,

Dersten sonra
bira içelim mi?
Görüşürüz.

Gül

b

Sevgili Dave,

Bu yaz
Istanbul'a
gidelim mi?

Asu

c

Sevgili Ayşegül,

Yarın partiye
gidiyor muyuz?

Andy

d

Yeşim,

Bu pazar yüzmeye
gidelim mi?

Ahmet

i

Andy,

Yarın
meşgulüm
sevgilim.

Ayşegül

ii

İyi fikir.

Kafede
görüşürüz.

Suzan

iii

Sevgili Ahmet,

Harika bir fikir gidelim.
Hava da çok sıcak.

Sevgiler

Yeşim

iv

Çok iyi fikir.

Cumartesi biletleri
alalım.

Dave

▶ 4 Write the following digital times in full, then convert them into 12-hour clock format. The first one has been done for you. Listen to them on the recording and repeat them out loud.

Saat kaç?	24-hour clock	12-hour clock
a 12.30	oniki otuz	yarım
b 15.15	....	....
c 08.50	....	....
d 04.25	....	....
e 18.45	....	....
f 09.10	....	....
g 24.00	....	....
h 10.10	....	....
i 05.05	....	....
j 13.02	....	....

5 Translate the following into Turkish.

a It's five past two.
b At twenty-five to three.
c At a quarter past four.
d It's a quarter to seven.
e At half past twelve.
f It's ten to eight.
g At twenty-five past seven
h It's a quarter past eleven.
i It's a quarter to ten.
j At five past nine.

6 Add the -de / -da endings to the following words. Remember to use -de / -da according to the rules of vowel harmony and also to make any necessary consonant changes, e.g. d to t where necessary.

a Sinema
b Tiyatro
c İş
d Park
e Otobüs
f Tren
g Vapur
h Dolmuş
i Uçak
j Durak
k Otel

7 Write two short dialogues.

a You are going past a cinema. There is a very good film on, which you would like to see. Suggest to your friend that you go and see the film together. Your friend politely refuses the suggestion. Re-order the following sentences to form a meaningful dialogue.

i Ne zaman?
ii Bu Cumartesi.
iii Sinemaya gidelim mi?
iv Özür dilerim. Meşgulüm.

b You are going past a tea garden in Turkey. It's hot and you are very thirsty. Suggest to your friend that you stop and have a drink. Your friend enthusiastically accepts the suggestion. Re-order the following sentences to form a meaningful dialogue.

i Köşede. Kafede.
ii Nerede?
iii Çok iyi fikir. Hadi gidelim ve soğuk bir şey içelim.
iv Çok sıcak, soğuk bir şey içelim mi?

8 Reading passage

The Bosporus is the channel between the Black Sea and the Aegean and it also separates the two continents of Asia and Europe. If you take a boat tour along the Bosporus in Istanbul, you zigzag between continents!

Read the passage and timetable to get the gist of it. Don't worry if you don't understand every word. Read the passage a couple of times and try to answer the following questions.

a Where do the boats leave from daily?
b How many boats leave daily and at what time?
c At how many places does the boat stop?
d How long does it stop for at Anadolu Kavağı?

Boğaz gezi vapuru *Boat trips on the Bosporus*
Vapurumuz Eminönü'nden hergün saat 10.35, 12.00 ve 13.35'te kalkıyor. Özel Boğaz Gezisi Vapuru'muz sırasıyla, Barbaros Hayrettin Paşa, Kanlıca, Emirgan, Yeniköy, Sarıyer, Rumeli Kavağı iskelelerinde duruyor ve Anadolu Kavağı son iskeledir. Vapurumuz her seferinde Anadolu Kavağı'nda 2–3 saat kalmaktadır. Burada çok güzel balık lokantaları vardır.

Ayrıca, cumartesi, pazar ve Bayram günleri saat 10.35 ile 13.35 vapurlarımızda canlı müzik vardır.

GİDİŞ				DÖNÜŞ			
EMİNÖNÜ Kalkış	10.35	12.00	13.35	A. KAVAĞI Kalkış	15.00	16.15	17.00
B. H. PAŞA	10.50	12.15	13.50	R. KAVAĞ	15.10	16.00	17.10
KANLICA	11.15	12.40	14.15	SARIYER	15.20	16.25	17.20
EMİRGAN	11.25	12.50	14.25	YENİKÖY	15.35	16.40	17.35
YENİKÖY	11.40	13.05	14.40	EMİRGAN	15.50	16.50	17.50
SARIYER	11.55	13.20	14.55	KANLICA	16.00	17.00	1800
R. KAVAĞI	12.05	13.45	15.05	B. H. PAŞA	16.25	17.25	18.25
A. KAVAĞI Varış	12.15	13.35	15.15	EMİNÖNÜ Varış	16.35	17.35	18.35

gidiş	going	kalkış	leaving
dönüş	return	varış	arriving / arrival

For more information go to the Turkish Maritime Organization (**Türkiye Denizcilik İşletmeleri A.Ş.**) website at: **www.tdi.com.tr**

9 In the left-hand column someone is saying they have a problem, or need help. The right-hand column contains offers of help. Match the two together.

a Acıktım.
b Burası çok sıcak.
c Program güzel değil.
d Telefon çalıyor.
e Sıkıldım.
f Valiz çok ağır.
g Başım ağrıyor.
h Yağmur yağıyor.
i Çok güneş.
j Yorgunum.
k Program sıkıcı.
l Uçak pahalı.

i Ben taşıyayım mı?
ii Sana tost yapayım mı?
iii Televizyonu kapatayım mı?
iv Pencereyi açayım mı?
v Müzik koyayım mı?
vi Cevap vereyim mi?
vii Trenle gidelim.
viii Sana Aspirin vereyim mi?
ix Şemsiyeyi alalım.
x Gölgede oturalım.
xi Tatile gidelim.
xii Televizyonu kapatalım mı?

10 Here is an authentic environmental message taken from a Turkish newspaper. Translate it into English then check your answer at the back of the book. To help you find verbs in your dictionary:

- take the verb stem,
- add -**mek** or -**mak** to form the verb's dictionary form,
- now look it up in the dictionary.

> **Yeşili**
> **sevelim**
> **ormanları**
> **koruyalım.**

▶ 11 Pronunciation: u, ü, v. First, listen to the recording, then listen while looking at the following sounds, finally listen and repeat.

u	ü	v
uç	üç	av
ud	süt	ev
bu	güç	var
su	tüy	ver

▶ Mini-test

Well done; you have now completed Unit 9! Now you will be able to make arrangements to go out or suggest doing something, you'll be able to buy tickets for transport, you'll be able to tell the time, book a seat at a theatre or cinema and make and accept or refuse an invitation. Give yourself a point for each of the following things that you can say in Turkish without looking at the book.

1 Suggest going to the theatre as there's a good play on.
2 Ask for two return tickets to Istanbul.
3 Say and write out 15.15 in words using the 12-hour clock format.
4 Ask the time.
5 Book a seat at a cinema for this Sunday.

Points:_____/5

10

how was it?

In this unit you will learn
- how to talk about the past,
  including your experiences
  and historical facts
- how to write a postcard
- how to have a social chat
- pronunciation: **y, z**

▶ Dialogue 1 The holiday was wonderful!

Yasemin's mother is Turkish, her father is English, she was born and brought up in England. She speaks very good Turkish. She is being interviewed by a Turkish TV presenter for a holiday programme.

Presenter İyi günler, Yasemin Hanım.
Yasemin İyi günler. Bana Yasemin deyin, lütfen.
Presenter Tatiliniz nasıldı?
Yasemin Harikaydı. Her gün güneşliydi. Bütün hafta hiç yağmur yağmadı.
Presenter Deniz?
Yasemin Sakin ve masmaviydi. Su ılıktı. Her gün yüzdük, sandalda kürek çektik ve kumlarda yürüdük.
Presenter Ya otel, otel nasıldı?
Yasemin Çok rahattı, oda deniz manzaralıydı ve servis çok iyiydi.
Presenter Yemekler?
Yasemin Ah, yemekler harikaydı. Türk yemekleri yapmayı öğreniyorum. Çoban-salatası çok yararlı ve lezzetli. Dün, Türk kahvesi yaptım ve arkadaşım fal baktı. Her şey çok güzeldi, gelecek tatil için odamı ayırttım bile. Ben burada bir ev almak istiyorum.

Questions

1 Tatil nasıldı?
2 Deniz nasıldı?
3 Tatilde ne yaptılar?
4 Otel nasıldı?
5 Yemekler nasıldı?

bana Yasemin deyin	call me Yasemin
tatiliniz nasıldı?	how was your holiday?
harikaydı	it was wonderful
bütün	all
hiç	(not) at all
hiç yağmur yağmadı	it never rained
sakin	calm
masmavi	very blue, intense blue, crystal blue
ılıktı	it was warm
yüzmek	to swim
sandal	rowing boat
kürek çekmek	to row a boat

kumlar	sand
yürümek	to walk
servis	service
çoban-salatası	mixed salad (lit. Shepherd's salad)
yararlı	good for you
yapmak	to make / to do
dün	yesterday
arkadaşım	my friend
fal bakmak	to read fortunes
gelecek	next
ayırtmak	to book
bile	even

Language points

The past form of verbs

To talk about the past, you need to learn one simple past tense in Turkish. You use the same form of the verb to talk about things which happened and have happened.

You can spot the past tense by an ending which includes **-di**. To make a past tense form you put **-dı, -di, -du** or **-dü** endings after nouns, adjectives and verbs (or **-tı, -ti, -tu** or **-tü** after the hard consonants **ç, f, h, k, p, s, ş** or **t**). The good news is that almost all Turkish verbs follow these rules.

To make the simple past tense of a verb you take the following steps:

Action	**Example**	
• take the infinitive of the verb,	yürümek	*to walk*
• take the stem of the verb,	yürü	*walk*
• add the past form of the verb *to be*.	yürü**düm**	*I walked*

Here are some more examples:

	sevmek *to love*	**almak** *to buy/take*	**durmak** *to stop*	**yüzmek** *to swim*
ben	sev**dim**	al**dım**	dur**dum**	yüz**düm**
sen	sev**din**	al**dın**	dur**dun**	yüz**dün**
o	sev**di**	al**dı**	dur**du**	yüz**dü**
biz	sev**dik**	al**dık**	dur**duk**	yüz**dük**
siz	sev**diniz**	al**dınız**	dur**dunuz**	yüz**dünüz**
onlar	sev**diler**	al**dılar**	dur**dular**	yüz**düler**

To make a verb in the past tense **negative** (*did not*), add -**me** or -**ma** onto the stem of the verb before the -**di** ending.

ben	sevmedim	almadım	durmadım	yüzmedim
sen	sevmedin	almadın	durmadın	yüzmedin
o	sevmedi	almadı	durmadı	yüzmedi
biz	sevmedik	almadık	durmadık	yüzmedik
siz	sevmediniz	almadınız	durmadınız	yüzmediniz
onlar	sevmediler	almadılar	durmadılar	yüzmediler

To make a verb in the past tense into a question (*did I ...?*) add -**mı**, -**mi**, -**mu** or -**mü** *after* the -**di** and the personal endings.

ben	sevdim mi?	aldım mı?	durdum mu?	yüzdüm mü?
sen	sevdin mi?	aldın mı?	durdun mu?	yüzdün mü?
o	sevdi mi?	aldı mı?	durdu mu?	yüzdü mü?
biz	sevdik mi?	aldık mı?	durduk mu?	yüzdük mü?
siz	sevdiniz mi?	aldınız mı?	durdunuz mu?	yüzdünüz mü?
onlar	sevdiler mi?	aldılar mı?	durdular mı?	yüzdüler mi?

▶ Dialogue 2 The holiday was a disaster!

An unhappy tourist is being interviewed by a Turkish TV presenter for a holiday programme.

Presenter Tatiliniz nasıldı?
Tourist Berbattı. Herşey herşey çok kötüydü.
Presenter Hava nasıldı?
Tourist Önce çok sıcaktı sonra rüzgarlı ve yağmurluydu.
Presenter Ya deniz?
Tourist Berbattı. Deniz soğuk ve çok dalgalıydı.
Presenter Otel? Nerede kaldınız? Otel nasıldı?
Tourist Otel çok gürültülüydü. Önümüzde bir inşaat vardı, bütün manzarayı kapatıyordu. Açık disko çok yakındı ve müzik çok yüksekti. Yatak sertti, duş bozuktu.
Presenter Yemekleri sevdiniz mi?
Tourist Ah, yemekler berbattı, lezzetsizdi. Sebze ve meyveler taze değildi. Çatal, bıçak da hiç temiz değildi. Servis çok yavaştı. Herşey çok pahalıydı ve de çok kötüydü. Kız arkadaşım da beni bıraktı gitti. Tatilim berbat oldu.
During the interview the tourist is stung by a bee.
Tourist Ahh! Arı soktu!

Questions

1 Hava iyi miydi?
2 Deniz nasıldı?
3 Otel çok iyiydi, değil mi?
4 Yemekler nasıldı?

berbat	*terrible*
herşey	*everything*
herşey herşey	*absolutely everything*
kötü	*bad*
önce	*at first*
sonra	*later*
dalgalı	*rough*
kalmak	*to stay*
gürültü	*noise*
gürültülüydü	*it was noisy*
önümüzde	*in front of us*
inşaat	*building site*
açık disko	*open-air disco*
sert	*hard*
bozuktu	*out of order*
çatal	*fork*
bıçak	*knife*
kötüydü	*it was bad*
berbat oldu	*it is ruined*
arı	*bee*
sokmak	*to sting*
arı soktu!	*I've been stung by a bee!* (lit. a bee has stung me!)

Language points

The past form of 'to be'

You can add the past tense endings of the verb *to be* to nouns, adjectives and adverbs to describe how things were. Here are some examples:

Present tense	Past tense
ben rahatım *I am comfortable*	rahattım* *I was comfortable*
sen rahatsın	rahattın
o rahat	rahattı
biz rahatız	rahattık
siz rahatsınız	rahattınız
onlar rahatlar	rahattılar or rahatlardı
ben iyiyim** *I'm fine / good*	iyiydim *I was fine / good*
sen iyisin	iyiydin
o iyi	iyiydi
biz iyiyiz	iyiydik
siz iyisiniz	iyiydiniz
onlar iyiler	iyiydiler or iyilerdi

*Remember, **d** becomes **t** after **t** as in **rahattım**.
Connecting **y used between vowels, as in **iyiyim** and **iyiydim**.

You say *was not* or *were not* by using the word **değil** with the endings used above. For example:

Negatives in the present tense	Negatives in the past tense
ben iyi değilim *I'm not well*	ben iyi değildim *I wasn't well*
sen iyi değilsin	sen iyi değildin
o iyi değil	o iyi değildi
biz iyi değiliz	biz iyi değildik
siz iyi değilsiniz	siz iyi değildiniz
onlar iyi değiller	onlar iyi değillerdi *or* değildiler

You use **-mı**, **-mi**, **-mu**, or **-mü** to make the sentence a question.

Questions in the present tense	Questions in the past tense
Harika mıyım? *Am I wonderful?*	Harika mıydım? *Was I wonderful?*
Harika mısın?	Harika mıydın?
Harika mı?	Harika mıydı?
Harika mıyız?	Harika mıydık?
Harika mısınız?	Harika mıydınız?
Harikalar mı?/Onlar harika mı?	Harikalar mıydı? / (Harika mıydılar?)

Reading comprehension: The postcard

Su is on holiday in Turkey. She stayed on the island for a week then came to Istanbul where she wrote this postcard. Pay particular attention to the use of tenses.

Sevgili Anneciğim,

Tatil harika geçiyor. Her sabah simit yiyorum. Üç kere deveye bindim. Henüz rakı içmedim. Hava hergün güneşli. Bir hafta adada kaldık, şimdi İstanbul'dayız. Dün Topkapı'ya gittik ama henüz Ayasofya'yı gezmedik. Sana bir kilo lokum aldım. On gündür tavla öğreniyorum. Çok mutluyum. Yakında görüşürüz.

Sevgilerimle

Su

xx

Questions

Answer the questions below and then check them with the answers at the back of the book.

1 Su hiç rakı içti mi?
2 Su şimdi adada mı?
3 Su Ayasofya'yı gezdi mi?

Language points

Using the past tense

Turkish does not have an equivalent of the English tense *have done* (present perfect). Instead, you often use the past tense, for example:

Arı soktu!	*A bee has stung me!*
Hiç ayran içtin mi?	*Have you ever drunk ayran?*
İstanbul'a hiç gitmedim.	*I haven't been to Istanbul.*
Ayasofya'ya gittin mi?	*Have you been to St Sophia?*

In some cases you use the Turkish -iyor tense to translate the English *have done* tense (see *Teach Yourself Turkish*, Unit 5 for more examples).

Where English uses a present tense (something ongoing) note that Turks sometimes use the past tense. In conversations you are likely to hear the following:

Phrase	Literal translation	Meaning
Efendim, anlamadım.	*Pardon, I didn't understand you.*	*I don't understand you.*
sıkıldım	*I was bored*	*I'm bored*
acıktım	*I was hungry*	*I'm hungry*
susadım	*I was thirsty*	*I'm thirsty*
yoruldum	*I got tired*	*I'm tired*
yolumu kaybettim	*I lost my way*	*I'm lost*
geç kaldım	*I was late*	*I'm late*
geldim	*I came*	*I'm coming, I've come, I'll be right there*
memnun oldum	*I became glad*	*I'm glad, I'm pleased*

Past time expressions

dün	*yesterday*
dün akşam	*yesterday evening*
dün gece	*last night*
geçen hafta	*last week*
geçen hafta sonu	*last weekend*
geçen ay	*last month*
iki saat önce	*two hours ago*
geçen yıl/sene	*last year*

▶ Listening comprehension: Guess who?

Listen to this biography of a famous American. It is written in the past tense. How many clues do you need to guess this person's identity? Listen as many times as you need before looking at the transcript in the back of the book. Then answer the questions.

1 Kim?
2 Askerlik yaptı mı?
3 Kimle evlendi?

4 Yakışıklı mıydı?
5 Mesleği neydi?
6 Ünlü müydü?
7 Siz onu hiç dinlediniz mi?

doğmak	to be born
ilk	first
kez	time
plak	record
anlaşmak	to sign a contract
TV'ye çıkmak	to be on TV
askerlik	military service
askerliğini yaptı	did his military service
... ile evlenmek	to get married to ...
boşanmak	to divorce
arası	between
konser vermek	to give a concert
ölmek	to die
...'den fazla	more than ...
müzikal	musical
oynamak	to act
ödül	award
altın	gold
platin	platinum
kral	king

⒤ Atatürk, Mustafa Kemal

Mustafa Kemal Atatürk was the founder of the Turkish Republic and as such he is still a key figure in modern Turkey. Under his leadership, Turkish society was transformed radically. Today you will find his statue in every town square and his portrait in schools and offices and on banknotes and stamps.

When Mustafa Kemal was a young man, at the end of the 19th century, Turkey was part of the decaying Ottoman Empire, which had been ruled for 600 years as an Islamic state by autocratic sultans. Atatürk's vision was to modernize Turkey and he looked towards Western Europe for models of democratic, secular government.

After the First World War, and the abdication of the last Sultan, Turkey became an autonomous state in 1923 with Atatürk as its leader. Atatürk started his reforms by establishing a parliamentary democracy, then began a cultural revolution. He wanted to abolish the culture and customs of the Islamic Ottoman society. He replaced the Arabic alphabet with the Roman alphabet; the Islamic calendar with the western calendar; the Friday 'day of rest' was moved to Sunday. He reformed the dress code for men and women, outlawing the veil and the fez. He reformed the Turkish language. He promoted equality of the sexes, wanting men and women to socialize together. He separated religious affairs from politics, replacing Islamic law with a civil code, whilst upholding the right of the individual to follow their religion of choice.

Today Turkey is a member of NATO, and has for several years been seeking entry to the European Union. Following Atatürk's cultural and political revolution, Turkey is unique in being a secular Islamic country.

❶ Orhan Pamuk

The Turkish author Orhan Pamuk has won one of the world's richest book prizes, the International Impac Dublin Literary Award 2003. O. Pamuk's 1998 novel *Benim Adım Kırmız* (translated into English as *My Name is Red*) landed the €100,000 prize – the biggest for a single work of fiction in English.

❶ Cannes Festival winner

In 2003 the film **Uzak** *Distance* by Nuri Bilge Ceylan won the Grand Prize. The actors Muzaffer Özdemir and Mehmet E. Toprak won prizes for Best Actor.

Reading comprehension

Read the brief passage about Turkish history below and answer the questions. You do not need to know every word to be able to understand the passage. However, you will find key words in the vocabulary box and a translation of the passage at the back of the book. To reinforce the words and their past tense forms try Question 4 in the **Practice** section.

Türk tarihi *Turkish history*

Türkler Anadolu'ya Orta Asya'dan geldiler. Selçuk Türkleri 1071'de doğuda Malazgirt'ten Anadolu'ya girdi ve batıya yayıldı. Osman Bey Bursa'ya kadar geldi, sonra Bursa başkent oldu. 1453'te Fatih Sultan Mehmet Konstantinapol'u aldı ve

Osmanlı başkenti yaptı. Osmanlılar Orta Avrupa'da Viyana'da durdular. Osmanlılar Avrupa ve Anadolu'da çok güzel camiler, köprüler ve kervansaraylar yaptılar. Birinci Dünya Savaşı'ndan sonra İngiliz, Fransız, İtalyan ve Yunanlılar Türkiye'yi işgal ettiler. Atatürk Kurtuluş Savaşını kazandı. Türkiye Cumhuriyet oldu. Ankara başkent oldu. Atatürk ilk Türk Cumhurbaşkanı oldu ve çok devrimler yaptı.

Questions

1 Why is Sultan Mehmet important?
2 What is the Ottomans' contribution to the architecture of Europe and Anatolia?
3 According to the passage, in which three ways did Atatürk contribute to the history of Turkey?

tarih	*history*
Türk tarihi	*Turkish history*
Anadolu	*Anatolia*
Orta Asya	*Central Asia*
Selçuk Türkleri	*Seljuk*
Malazgirt	*Manzikert* (the name of a town)
girdi	*entered*
yayıldı	*spread*
Osman Bey	*Osman* (the head of the Ottoman clan)
Bursa'ya kadar	*as far as Bursa*
Fatih Sultan Mehmet	*Sultan Mehmet the conqueror*
aldı	*conquered, took*
Osmanlılar	*Ottomans*
Orta Avrupa'da	*Central Asia*
durdular	*stopped*
köprüler	*bridges*
kervansaraylar	*caravanserai* (inns with large courtyards)
Birinci Dünya Savaşı	*First World War*
...'dan sonra	*after ...*
işgal ettiler	*they occupied*
Kurtuluş Savaşı	*War of Independence*
kazandı	*won*
devrimler	*reforms*

Practice

▶ **1** You are a TV presenter who asked two holidaymakers (one happy, one unhappy) the same questions. Their answers got muddled up by the computer. Try to work out the answer each gave to each question.

a	İyi günler.	i	İyi günler.
b	Tatiliniz nasıldı?	ii	Çok iyiydi.
c	Hava nasıldı?	iii	Yemekler berbattı, lezzetsizdi.
d	Otel nasıldı?	iv	Otel çok gürültülüydü.
e	Yemekler nasıldı?	v	Çok rüzgarlı ve yağmurluydu.
		vi	Her gün güneşliydi.
		vii	Çok rahattı, oda deniz manzaralıydı.
		viii	Çok kötüydü.
		ix	Yemekler harikaydı.
		x	İyi günler.

2 Here are four situations where **A** says what he / she did and **B** asks questions about it. Match the statements with the questions.

i **A** Dün akşam sinemaya gittim.
   B ....

ii **A** Geçen pazar pideciye gittik.
   B ....

iii **A** Geçen hafta kitap aldım.
    B ....

iv **A** Hafta sonunda yüzdüm.
   B ....

> a Denizde mi, havuzda mı?
> b Hangi filmi gördün?
> c Hangi kitabı aldın?
> d Kimle gittin?

3 The verbs in the vocabulary box on the next page are in the dictionary (infinitive) form. Give their past forms. The first one has been done for you.

	ben	sen	o
doğmak	doğdum	doğdun	doğdu
anlaşmak			
TV'ye çıkmak			
plak yapmak			
evlenmek			
boşanmak			
konser vermek			
oynamak			
ödül almak			
ölmek			

4 Fill in the gaps. The following passage, taken from earlier in the unit, needs to have the correct verb endings inserted. They should all be in the past tense.

Türk tarihi
Türkler Anadolu'ya Orta Asya'dan 1 gel___. Selçuk Türkleri 1071'de doğuda Malazgirt'ten Anadolu'ya 2 gir___ ve batıya 3 yayıl___. Osman Bey Bursa'ya kadar 4 gel___, sonra Bursa başkent 5 ol___. 1453'te Fatih Sultan Mehmet Konstantinapol'u 6 al___ ve Osmanlı başkenti 7 yap___. Osmanlılar Orta Avrupa'da Viyana'da 8 dur___. Osmanlılar Avrupa ve Anadolu'da çok güzel camiler, köprüler ve kervansaraylar 9 yap___. Birinci Dünya Savaşı'ndan sonra İngiliz, Fransız, İtalyan ve Yunanlılar Türkiye'yi işgal 10 et___. Atatürk Kurtuluş Savaşını 11 kazan___. Türkiye Cumhuriyet 12 ol___. Ankara başkent 13 ol___. Atatürk ilk Türk Cumhurbaşkanı 14 ol___ ve çok devrimler 15 yap___.

5 Things you have or you haven't done.

tavla oynamak	*play backgammon*
nargile içmek	*smoke a hookah*
simit yemek	*eat simit* (bread in the shape of a ring)
deveye binmek	*ride a camel*
çamur banyosu yapmak	*to have a mud bath*
Ayasofya'yı gezmek	*to visit St Sophia*
hamama gitmek	*to go to a Turkish bath*
Karagöz ve Hacivat'ı seyretmek	*to watch Karagöz and Hacivat* (traditional puppet show)

Make up eleven questions, using the words above, to ask about things which you have / have not done. Use the present perfect tense.

Example Hiç rakı içtin mi? *Have you ever drunk raki?*

▶ 6 **Pronunciation: y, z.** Listen to the recording and repeat the following sounds until you feel comfortable with them.

y	z
ay	az
ye	iz
oy	oz
yi	zil
yıl	bizzz

7 Wordsearch. There are ten adjectives (describing words) for you to find.

H	A	R	İ	K	A	G	M	O	D
F	B	A	Y	S	T	Ü	A	P	A
R	E	H	İ	Z	H	R	S	E	L
K	C	A	L	S	K	Ü	M	K	G
B	M	T	I	E	T	L	A	P	A
E	H	K	B	R	D	T	V	A	L
R	M	R	N	T	A	Ü	İ	H	I
B	A	İ	H	İ	N	L	F	A	M
A	K	I	Ü	M	T	Ü	J	L	K
T	R	B	O	Z	U	K	B	I	Ü

▶ Mini-test

Well done. You have completed Unit 10. Now you will be able to talk about the past, past experiences and historical facts. You will also be able to write a postcard and have a short social chat. Give yourself a point for each of these things you can say in Turkish without looking at the book.

1 Ask someone how their holiday was.
2 Explain that your holiday was awful and everything went wrong.
3 Say that you have been to a Turkish bath.
4 Say that you have not had a mud bath.
5 Ask someone if they have ridden a camel.

Points:_____/5

Congratulations! You have completed *Teach Yourself Beginner's Turkish* and are now a competent speaker of basic Turkish. You should be able to handle most everyday situations on a visit to Turkey and to communicate with Turkish people sufficiently to make friends. If you would like to extend your ability so that you can develop your confidence, fluency and scope in the language, whether for social or business purposes, why not take your Turkish a step further with the full *Teach Yourself Turkish* course?

I hope that working your way through *Teach Yourself Beginner's Turkish* has been both a learning and enjoyable experience. If the course has provided you with what you wanted why don't you contact me and let me know what has worked well for you. If you think that the course could be improved I shall also be pleased to hear from you. All constructive comments and suggestions will be carefully looked at, and incorporated if possible into later editions.

You can contact me through the publishers at: Teach Yourself Books, Hodder Headline Ltd, 338 Euston Road, London NW1 3BH, UK

Good luck!

Asuman Çelen Pollard

taking it further

Now that you have completed the *Teach Yourself Beginner's Turkish* course, you may want to take your learning further. Here is some suggested reading: most of these resources should be available from libraries or bookshops in the English-speaking world.

More advanced Turkish language

- *Teach Yourself Turkish* (Hodder & Stoughton, 2003)

History, culture and literature

- *Harem: The World Behind the Veil*, A. L. Croutier (1998).
- *Culture Shock! Turkey: A Guide to Customs and Etiquette*, A. Bayraktaroğlu (2000).
- *Atatürk*, Andrew Mango (2001).
- *Mevlana – An Anthology of Translations of Mevlana Jalaluddin Rumi*, J. Rumi, K. Helminski (2000).
- *Turkish Delights*, P. Scott (2001).
- *Süleyman The Magnificent And His Age*, edited M. Kunt, C. Woodhead (1995).
- *The Book of Dede Korkut*, G. Lewis (2001).
- *Inside the Seraglio*, J. Freely (2000).
- *The Tales of Nasreddin Hodja*, Aziz Nesin (1996).

Travel guides

- *The Rough Guide to Turkey*, R. Ayliffe, M. Dubin, J. Gawthrop (2003).
- *Lonely Planet Turkey*, P. Yale, V. Campbell, R. Plunket (2003).

- *D. K. Eyewitness Travel Guide Turkey*, S. Swon (2003).
- *Explorer – Turkey*, D. Darke (1999).
- *A Let's Go Travel Guide – Turkey*, A. Cooley, K. Freeny, J. Greene, S. Lassman, C. Shepard, N. Waxman (2002).
- *Spiral Guide Turkish Coast*, L. Bennet, K. Gaild (2003).

Cookery books
- *Classic Turkish Cookery*, G. Başan (1998).
- *The Ottoman Kitchen*, S. Woodward (2001).

Websites

Tourism
- http://www.gototurkey.co.uk
- http://www.turizm.gov.tr

Weather forecasts
- http://www.meteor.gov.tr/webler/tahmin/tahminmaster.htm

Newspapers
- http://www.milliyet.com.tr
- http://www.radikal.com.tr
- http://www.sabah.com.tr
- http://www.turkishdailynews.com (a good English-language newspaper)

Maps
- http://mailgazete.com/turkharita/turkiye.htm (map of Turkey, city by city)

Chatline
- http://www.paltalk.com/www.sabah.com.tr

Ottoman history
- http://www.osmanlı.org.tr/

translations

Unit 1

Dialogue 1 Good evening

Hüseyin   Good evening, I'm Hüseyin. And you?
Ülkü   Good evening, I'm Ülkü.
Hüseyin   How are you, (Mrs) Ülkü? [**Hanım** is used after female names.]
Ülkü   Thanks, (Mr) Hüseyin. I'm fine. [**Bey** is used after male names.] How are you?
Hüseyin   I'm fine too.
Hüseyin   Wine?
Ülkü   Yes, please.

Dialogue 2 Hi, how are you?

Bahadır   Hello Ülkü, how are you?
Ülkü   I'm fine, thanks. How are you?
Bahadır   I'm fine too.
Ülkü   Beer?
Bahadır   Yes, please.

Dialogue 3 It's a very nice party

Ülkü   Good evening, I'm Ülkü. And you?
Banu   Good evening, I'm Banu.
Ülkü   How are you, Banu?
Banu   Thanks, I'm fine.
Ülkü   It's a very good party, isn't it?
Banu   Yes, it is.
Ülkü   Banu, (this is) Doktor Bahadır Bey.

Dialogue 4 Goodbye

Bahadır   Good evening.
Banu   Good evening, (Mr) Bahadır.
Bahadır   How are you, Banu?
Banu   Thanks, I'm fine. How are you?

Bahadır	I'm fine too.
Banu	Goodbye, (Mrs) Ülkü. Goodbye, (Mr) Bahadır. Goodnight.
Ülkü and Bahadır	Goodbye, Banu.

Unit 2

Dialogue 1 A glass of tea, please

Waiter	How can I help you sir / madam?
Banu	A glass of tea, please.
Waiter	A glass of tea. For you, sir?
Şafak	A beer and a bottle of water, please.
Waiter	There isn't any beer, sir.
Şafak	What is there to drink?
Waiter	Here you are, the menu.
Şafak	Thanks. One coffee, please.
Waiter	Milk?
Şafak	Yes, with milk.
Waiter	A tea and a coffee with milk?
Şafak	Yes, OK.
Waiter	Tea, coffee, milk and sugar.
Banu and Şafak	Thanks.
Waiter	Enjoy your drinks, sir / madam.
Şafak	Waiter!
Waiter	Yes, sir.
Şafak	The bill, please.
Şafak	Keep the change,
Waiter	Thank you, sir.

Dialogue 2 The coffee is very good here

Waiter	Yes, sir / madam.
Mother	One sweet coffee.
Father	A coffee for me too, without sugar.
Mother	You (my child) sweetheart? [**Yavrum** is a term of endearment used with a child.] Still lemonade?
Child	No, ayran.
Mother	OK.
Father	Two coffees, one with sugar, one without and an ayran.
Waiter	Yes, sir.
Waiter	Here you are, your drinks.
Everyone	Thanks.
Waiter	Enjoy your drinks.
Mother	The coffee is good, isn't it?
Father	Yes, very good.
Child	I'm hungry.
Mother	Me too. A toasted sandwich?
Child	Yes, a toasted cheese sandwich and an ayran.
Father	Waiter, please.
Waiter	Yes?

Father	Three toasted cheese sandwiches and three ayrans.
Mother	The view is beautiful, isn't it?
Father	Yes, very beautiful.

Dialogue 3 One red wine, please

Şafak	Good evening.
Waiter	Good evening, sir / madam. How can I help you?
Banu	A glass of wine, please.
Şafak	Red or white?
Banu	Red, please.
Şafak	A glass of red wine and a glass of raki, please.
Waiter	Of course, sir. Snacks?
Şafak	Yes, nuts and some mixed fruit and white cheese, please.
Waiter	Of course, sir.

Unit 3

Dialogue 1 Which hotel?

Ben	Hello.
Clerk	Hello, sir.
Ben	Have you got an accommodation list, please?
Clerk	Hotels, guest houses or campsites?
Ben	Hotels, please.
Clerk	Here you are.
Ben	Which hotel is near by?
Clerk	Yeşil Ev is very near.
Ben	How do you spell it, please?
Clerk	Y–e–ş–i–l E–v.
Ben	Thanks.
Clerk	Here is the map, this is the information office and this is 'Yeşil Ev.'
Ben	Oh! Wonderful, thank you very much.
Ben	I wonder which building it is.
Laura	I think it's that building.
Ben	Yes, that's the building.

Dialogue 2 Do you have a vacant room?

Ben	Good evening.
Receptionist	Good evening, sir, madam.
Ben	Do you have a vacant room?
Receptionist	For how many people?
Ben	Me and my sister, two single rooms.
Receptionist	Unfortunately, we do not have two single rooms. But we do have one big room with two single beds.
Receptionist	There is a balcony and a sea view.
Laura	Is there a bath and hot water?
Receptionist	Yes. There is both a bath and a shower. There is hot water 24 hours.

Ben	This room is beautiful, isn't it?
Laura	Yes. How much?
Receptionist	$120.
Laura	Is breakfast included?
Receptionist	Yes, it is included.
Laura	Yes. Fine.
Receptionist	How many nights?
Ben	Three nights.
Receptionist	Passports, please?
Ben	Of course, here they are.
Receptionist	Thanks.
Receptionist	Place of birth ... date of birth ... nationality ... passport number ... Room number 24
Receptionist	Here is the key.
Laura	Suitcases?
Receptionist	Mehmet!

Dialogue 3 There are lots of good campsites

Şafak	Hi.
Clerk	Good morning. (Good day.)
Şafak	Have you got a list of hotels and campsites?
Clerk	Yes. This is the hotel list.
Banu	The hotels are a bit expensive.
Clerk	There are lots of good campsites and they are very cheap. Here is the list with the addresses and the telephone numbers.
Banu	Is there a public phone near here?
Clerk	Yes. There is one over there.
Şafak	Have you got any telephone cards?
Clerk	Yes, 10 million lira.
Şafak	One card, please.
Kamp	Hello ... 752 52 06 Truva campsite. Yes?
Şafak	Hello. This is Şafak Gezer. Have you got a tent for two?
Kamp	Yes, we have. For how many days?
Şafak	Five days.
Kamp	Fine.
Şafak	What facilities does the campsite have? Is there any electricity?
Kamp	Certainly. There is electricity, water and hot water all the time. There is a restaurant, swimming pool, beach, showers, a play area for children, first aid post and also a public telephone.
Şafak	Fine. See you tomorrow morning.
Kamp	OK. Your name, please?
Şafak	My first name is Şafak, surname Gezer.
Kamp	Pardon? How do you spell it?
Şafak	Ş – a – f – a – k G – e – z – e – r.

Dialogue 4 This is your tent.

Ayşegül	I'm Ayşegül. Welcome.
Banu	I'm Banu. This is Şafak.
Banu and Şafak	Hoş bulduk. (The set reply to 'Welcome'.)
Ayşegül	How are you?
Banu	We're fine, thanks. How are you?
Ayşegül	Very busy.
Ayşegül	This is your tent, here is the car park, this is the telephone, that (place) is the swimming pool and that is the restaurant, these are the toilets, those are the showers, this is the first aid post.
Ayşegül	And that is our dog, 'Karabaş'.

Unit 4

Dialogue 1 Ordering breakfast

Laura	Breakfast in the garden is very pleasant.
Ben	Yes. What beautiful weather!
Waiter	Good morning, sir, madam.
Ben	Good morning. We'd like Turkish breakfast, please.
Waiter	Of course, sir.
Laura	What is there for breakfast?
Waiter	Butter, honey, marmalade, jam, cheese, olives, sausages.
Ben	Have you got any Turkish sausages?
Waiter	We do, sir. We also have salami, tomatoes, cucumber, pepper. And fresh bread of course.
Ben	Do you have tea?
Waiter	Of course.
Laura	Thanks.
Laura	The tea is delicious (very tasty).
Waiter	Enjoy your meal.
Waiter	Egg?
Laura	No, thanks.
Ben	Yes, soft boiled for me, please.
Waiter	Of course, sir.
Ben	The Turkish spicy sausage is very tasty.
Laura	Isn't there any salt?
Ben	Here it is on the table, dear.
Waiter	Here is the toast. Enjoy your meal. Anything else?
Laura	No, thanks.

Dialogue 2 At a fish restaurant

Ahmet	Waiter, please.
Waiter	Yes, sir.
Ahmet	What wines do you suggest (are there)?
Waiter	Çankaya and Kutman are very good.
Yeşim	Çankaya, please.
Asuman	For me white Çankaya, please.

Ahmet	What about you, Vanessa?
Vanessa	(Sour) cherry juice, please.
Ahmet	One large, white Çankaya, one small rakı, one (sour) cherry juice.
Waiter	Straight away, sir.
Ahmet	And a bottle of water.
Ahmet	For me fried turbot and mixed salad, please.
Asuman	For me steamed bass and green salad, please.
Vanessa	For me fried mullet with sliced tomatoes, please.
Yeşim	For me grilled blue fish and rocket, please.
Waiter	Of course, sir.
Ahmet	Waiter, the bill, please.
Waiter	Here you are, the bill.
Ahmet	Thanks. Keep the change.
Waiter	Thank you, sir.
Ahmet	Where is the taxi?
Waiter	Here, on the right, sir.

Dialogue 3 At a *köfte* restaurant

Ben	The pudding shop or the meatball restaurant?
Laura	Noon, meatball restaurant; evening, pudding shop.
Ben	OK. Come on.
Ben	Have you got meatballs?
Waiter	Yes, sir. How many portions?
Laura	Two portions, with cooked rice.
Waiter	Of course, madam.
Laura to Ben	Are you drinking beer, or ayran?
Ben	Is the beer cold?
Waiter	Yes, very cold.
Ben	For me, a cold beer.
Laura	And for me, chilled ayran.
Waiter	Anything else? (lit. What else?)
Ben	Have you got white bean salad?
Waiter	Yes, we have, sir.
Ben	I'll have the bean salad (lit. For me).
Laura	And for me a mixed salad.
Waiter	Enjoy your meals.
Ben and Laura	Thanks.
Laura	The meatballs are very very tasty, aren't they?
Ben	Yes, they are.

Unit 5

Dialogue 1 At the airport

Bahadır	Excuse me, where is the bank, please? [Using **siz** – polite – form.]
Passer-by	I am sorry. I don't know. Ask at the information desk. The information office is over there.

Bahadır	Thank you very much.
Ülkü	Excuse me, where is the bank, please?
Clerk	Go straight ahead, pass passport control and after customs turn right, go straight ahead again, it is on the left.
Ülkü	Ah, thank you very much. Where are the nearest toilets, please?
Clerk	Go straight ahead: there are two toilets before passport control, one on the right and one on the left. After passport control there are two more toilets.
Bahadır	Thank you very much.
Clerk	Not at all.
Bahadır	Where are the taxis, please?
Clerk	Go out of the door, cross the road, and they are there.
Driver	Where to, sir, madam?
Bahadır	Sultan Ahmet, please. Is Sultan Ahmet far?
Driver	Quite – 20 kilometres, approximately 40 minutes.

Dialogue 2 In Sultan Ahmet Square

Ülkü	Excuse me, where is the Topkapı Museum, please?
Passer-by	Pardon?
Ülkü	Where is the Topkapı Museum, please?
Passer-by	I am sorry, I don't know.
Ülkü	Excuse me, where is the Topkapı, please?
Passer-by	Go straight on, turn right at the corner and it is right opposite you.
Ülkü	When are the museums open?
Passer-by	From 9 to 5 o'clock.
Ülkü	Thanks.
Passer-by	Not at all.
Bahadır	Two tickets, please.
Receptionist	Here you are. You can leave your bags here.
Bahadır	Thanks. Where is the Harem?
Receptionist	Go straight ahead. There are signs over there.

Dialogue 3 Blue Cruise

Ülkü	Excuse me, are there Blue Cruises from Bodrum?
Clerk	Yes, there are.
Ülkü	Where do they go? (lit. Where to?)
Clerk	One goes from Bodrum to Ören, from Ören to Körmen, then from Körmen back to Bodrum. A second goes from Bodrum to Karaada, from Karaada to Cedre, from Cedre to Ballısu, from Ballısu to Bodrum.
Ülkü	Aaa! The first one sounds good. Where is the port?
Clerk	On the coast, in the centre (of the coast).
Ülkü	Thanks.
Clerk	Not at all.

Unit 6

Dialogue 1 At a travel agency

Anne What places are hot in Turkey?

Travel agent The south is very hot in August and July. It's warm in spring, hot in June.

Anne We like it very hot. We don't like rain. And (the) children like the sea and sand.

Travel agent In July Alanya is 26°C, Antalya 28°C, Bodrum 27°C, Fethiye 27°C, Istanbul 23°C. In July, Antalya is the hottest. There is no rain in the summer in the south. The weather is sunny all the time. In the spring mostly there are spring rains and later (there is) a rainbow. In the countryside there is a variety of beautiful wild flowers.

Anne Yes. Which days are there flights (lit. aeroplanes) to Antalya?

Travel agent Monday, Wednesday, Friday there is a flight a day. Saturdays and Sundays there are two aeroplanes a day.

Anne Are there seats Sunday 5th May?

Travel agent Yes, there are. For how many people?

Dialogue 2 We like different things

Cem Gökhan and I like football, basketball, volleyball and tennis.

Gökhan But we like football most.

Vanessa We like the sea, dancing and day trips. What a nice day without rain and wind.

Cem My parents like day trips, especially visiting ruins. Eating in restaurants is very enjoyable. Don't stand there, there is a lot of sun, come into the shade. Waiter, a chocolate ice cream for me.

Vanessa Plain ice cream for me.

Cem Fruit flavoured for me.

Çiğdem Lemon flavoured for me.

Gökhan Mixed for me.

Waiter OK, sir / madam.

Reading comprehension

Seasons and climate in Turkey

There are four seasons in Turkey: spring, summer, autumn and winter. The climate is different (in) each season.

In the Mediterranean, Aegean and Marmara regions summers are hot and dry, winters are warm and wet (rainy). There is snow on the very high mountains. The coasts are warmer in Turkey. In Istanbul and Marmara the average temperature (in winter) is 4°C, and in summer 27°C.

In the Black Sea region summers are hot. Winters are cooler in the south. Sometimes it is frosty and there is snow in every season. The average temperature in summer is 23°C and in winter 7°C. The most rainfall falls in Rize.

In Central Anatolia the difference in temperature between day and night is very great. Summers are less hot (cooler). In the summer the average temperature is 23°C, in winter −2°C. In the south-east of Anatolia summers are very hot, winters are less cold (warm).

In the south while you are on the sand (beach) there is snow on the Taurus Mountains.

Exercise 3

Ali is taller than Betül, but Ali is shorter than Can. Dursun is shorter than Can. Who is the shortest?

Unit 7

Dialogue 1 Where are you from?

Woman	Hello.
Man	Hello.
Woman	Where are you from?
Man	I'm from Leeds. Where are you from?
Woman	I'm German. From Bonn.
Man	I'm English but my wife (partner) is Turkish, from Istanbul. This book is for learning Turkish, *Teach Yourself Turkish*. I speak Turkish and German, French, Spanish, Italian, and a little Bulgarian. I like Turkish people, (the) language and Turkey very much. Our daughter Vanessa also speaks (lit. knows) Turkish.
Woman	Really? Very interesting.
Man	We love going (lit. It's very enjoyable to go) to Turkey for holidays. We are very lucky, Turks are very friendly and honest, aren't they?
Woman	Yes, you're right.

Dialogue 2 Are you Turkish?

Susie	Hello, I'm Susie. And you?
Ayda	I'm Ayda.
Susie	Are you Turkish?
Ayda	Yes. And you? Are you American?
Susie	No. I'm English. I'm from London.
Ayda	Are you a model?
Susie	No, I'm a student. And you?
Ayda	I'm a doctor.

Susie	You must be (lit. are) very clever.
Ayda	I'm not very clever but I'm very hard working.
Susie	Are you married?
Ayda	No, I'm engaged. You?
Susie	I'm single, I'm only 23 years old. Is your fiancé handsome?
Ayda	Cem is tall, dark, black-haired, dark-brown eyed (lit. black eyed), and of course in my opinion very handsome. He is very clever and a very good person. He is an engineer and we're very good friends.

Dialogue 3 How are you?

Ülkü	Hello!
Gonca	Hello. Ülkü, is that you?
Ülkü	Yes, it's me. (Sister) Gonca, is that you?
Gonca	Yes, it's me, dear. How are you?
Ülkü	Thank you, I am fine. How are you?
Gonca	I'm fine.

Dialogue 4   Hello?

Banu	Hello?
Şafak	Hello, Banuş, this is Şafak.
Banu	Hello, Şaf. How are you?
Şafak	I'm fine.

Unit 8

Dialogue 1 Planning the day

Ben	What are we doing today?
Laura	I don't know. I want to buy presents.
Ben	And I want to buy a leather jacket, shoes and Turkish delight.
Laura	Shall we go to the Grand Bazaar. Blouse, bag, spices, shoes and things for presents.
Ben	Where shall we go?
Laura	I want to go to the Grand Bazaar and Taksim.
Ben	OK. Let's go.

Dialogue 2 Buying bags

Laura	Hello.
Salesperson	Good day. Yes, madam.
Laura	How much are the leather bags?
Salesperson	The big one is 15, the medium-sized one is 10 and the small one 5 million lira.
Laura	That medium-sized one, please. 10 million is very expensive, is 4 million OK?
Salesperson	What colour?
Laura	Black, please.
Salesperson	Here you are. For you, 5 million.
Laura	OK.

Salesperson	Enjoy using it. (lit. use it in happy days.)
Laura	Thank you.

Dialogue 3 Buying spices

Stallholder	How can I help you?
Laura	We want to buy spices.
Stallholder	What kinds would you like to buy?
Laura	Spices for meatballs, cumin, sumac and such like.
Stallholder	How much?
Laura	In 100 gram packets.
Stallholder	Would you like something else?
Ben	What's this?
Stallholder	Sultan's medicated taffy.
Ben	What is Sultan's medicated taffy really?
Stallholder	It is an aphrodisiac.
Ben	I don't need it. I don't want it. (laughter) I'd like some dried fruit.
Stallholder	How much?
Ben	Half a kilo of apricots, half a kilo of figs. Have you got any hazelnuts. Are they good? Yes! Half a kilo of mixed nuts, please.
Ben	That's all. How much?
Stallholder	10 million. Very cheap. (lit. Cheaper than water.)

Dialogue 4 Buying Turkish delight

Laura	Where is the Haci Bekir Turkish delight shop, please?
Stallholder	Go straight ahead, turn right, it's on the left.
Laura	Thanks.
Stallholder	Not at all.
Shop assistant	How can I help you, madam?
Laura	We would like to buy some Turkish delight, how much is it?
Shop assistant	What kind?
Ben	What are there?
Shop assistant	This is mint flavoured, this is rose, this is plain, and this is nutty. Here you are. Let's 'eat sweet, talk sweet'. When we eat sweets we always say this.
Laura and Ben	Mmmm.
Shop assistant	Half a kilo mixed – 3 million liras.
Laura	Four half-kilo boxes of mixed, please.
Ben	Is the shop new?
Shop assistant	No, we have been making Turkish delight since 1777. Our Turkish delight is very fresh. We get fresh Turkish delight every day. Today we sell Turkish delight all over the world. We make different kinds every week.
Ben	How do you make it?
Shop assistant	We put sugar, nuts and ... but the recipe is our secret.

Ben	Do you sell Turkish delight mostly to tourists?
Shop assistant	No, we Turks give Turkish delight as a present when we visit each other on special days.

Dialogue 5 Buying clothes

Shop assistant	Yes, madam. How can I help you?
Laura	I'm looking for a blouse.
Shop assistant	What size?
Laura	38.
Shop assistant	Here you are. This blouse is very nice.
Laura	Green doesn't suit me. Do you have this in blue or white?
Shop assistant	Here you are. One blue, one white, size 38.
Laura	How much is it?
Shop assistant	58 million.
Laura	I would like to try them on.
Shop assistant	Of course.
Laura	I'll take this one. How much is it?
Shop assistant	58 million.
Laura	That's very expensive. I'll give you 40 million.
Shop assistant	We do not haggle here. To you, 50 million lira.
Laura	OK, I'll take it. (I'll buy it.)

Picture dictation

Suzan is sitting at a seaside café. She is looking at the people on the beach and in the sea, while drinking fruit juice. Three children are buying ice-cream. A couple are lying on the sand. The woman is wearing a hat and a bikini, and is reading a book. The man is wearing glasses and shorts, looking at the sea. In the sea there are a rowing boat and a sailing boat. There are seven people swimming.

Unit 9

Dialogue 1 What shall we do at the weekend?

Şafak	What shall we do at the weekend?
Banu	Shall we go to the theatre? There's a very good play on at (the) Kenterler.
Şafak	What's on?
Banu	Let's have a look. I think *Hep aşk Vardı* (*There has always been Love*) is on.
Şafak	*Hep aşk vardı* is on at 8.30.
Banu	Yes, wonderful. But I want to go to the cinema to see *Hamam* as well.
Şafak	So do I.
Banu	Should I give the Kenter a ring first?
Şafak	Yes, let's call them.
Şafak	What time is it?
Banu	Half past twelve. It's lunchtime.

Şafak	Let's call them again at half past one.
Banu	OK.

Dialogue 2 Booking seats at the theatre

Receptionist	How can I help you? 0212 246 35 89, the Kenter theatre.
Şafak	Good day. I would like to book two seats for *Hep aşk vardı* for this Sunday.
Receptionist	Good day, madam. Unfortunately there are no tickets for this Sunday but there are seats for the following Sunday.
Şafak	What are the prices?
Receptionist	Adult 15 million lira, student 5 million lira, concessions (lit. teacher and retired) 12 million.
Şafak	Two tickets, one adult and one student, please.
Receptionist	How are you paying? By card?
Şafak	Yes.
Receptionist	Card number, please?
Şafak	1234 1234 1234 1234.

Dialogue 3 Choosing a film to watch

Şafak	Are we going to the cinema this evening?
Banu	Let's see *Hamam*.
Şafak	Let's have a look at which films are on at the cinemas.
Banu	*Vampires* is on at (the) ABC cinema.
Şafak	I don't want to see a horror film.
Banu	*Şaban* is on at the Hisar.
Şafak	Isn't it a comedy?
Banu	Yes, but I want to see *Hamam*.
Şafak	What time?
Banu	It's on at five, seven and nine.
Şafak	Shall we go to the 7 o'clock one?
Banu	OK. Let's go now.
Şafak	The car has broken down. Are we going by dolmuş (shared taxi) or by bus? The bus is cheaper but the dolmuş is more comfortable.
Banu	It doesn't matter.
Şafak	Let's go by bus.

Dialogue 4 Buying bus tickets

Şafak	Two tickets to Taksim?
Banu	Buy them for the return journey as well.
Şafak	Four tickets, please.
Clerk	4 million lira.
Şafak	Here you are.
Clerk	Have you got any change?
Şafak	No, I haven't.
Clerk	Here you are. 6 million lira.

Exercise 8
Boat trips on the Bosporus
Our boat leaves Eminönü every day at 10.35, 12.00 and 13.35. The special Bosporus boat trip stops at the ports in this order: Barbaros, Hayrettin, Paşa, Kanlıca, Emirgan, Yeniköy, Sarıyer, Rumeli Kavağı; Anadolu Kavağı is the last port. Our boats stop (each time) at Anadolu Kavağı for two hours. There are very good fish restaurants there. And, on Saturdays, Sundays and Bayram days at 10.35 and 13.35 we have live music on the boat.

Unit 10

Dialogue 1   The holiday was wonderful!

Presenter	Good day, (Ms) Yasemin.
Yasemin	Good day. Please call me Yasemin.
Presenter	How was your holiday? (lit. How has your holiday been?)
Yasemin	It was wonderful. It was sunny every day. It didn't rain all week.
Presenter	What about the sea?
Yasemin	It was calm and very blue. The water was warm. Every day we swam, we rowed in a rowing boat and we walked on the sand.
Presenter	And the hotel, what was the hotel like?
Yasemin	It was very comfortable, the room had a view of the sea and the service was very good.
Presenter	And the food?
Yasemin	Ah, the dishes were wonderful. I'm learning how to cook Turkish dishes. The mixed salad (lit. Shepherd's salad) is very good for you and very tasty. Yesterday, I made Turkish coffee and my friend read the coffee cup (lit. read fortunes). Everything was very good, I've already booked my room for my next holiday. I want to buy a house here.

Dialogue 2   The holiday was a disaster!

Presenter	How was your holiday?
Tourist	Terrible. Absolutely everything went wrong (lit. was very bad).
Presenter	What was the weather like?
Tourist	At first it was too hot, later it was windy and rainy.
Presenter	What about the sea?
Tourist	It was terrible. The sea was cold and very rough.
Presenter	The hotel? Where did you stay? What was the hotel like?
Tourist	The hotel was very noisy. There was a building site in front of us, it blocked the whole view. An open-air disco

was very near and the music was very loud. The bed was hard, the shower was broken.

Presenter   Did you like the food?

Tourist   Oh, the food was terrible, it was tasteless. The vegetables and fruit were not fresh. The forks and knives were not clean (at all). The service was very slow. Everything was very expensive and very bad. My girlfriend left me. My holiday was a disaster.

Tourist   Ah! I've been stung!

Reading comprehension The postcard

Dear Mum,

I'm having a wonderful holiday. I've been eating simit every morning. I've ridden a camel three times. I haven't drunk any raki yet. The weather has been sunny every day. We stayed on the island for a week, now we are in Istanbul. We went to Topkapi yesterday but we haven't visited St. Sophia yet. I bought a kilo of Turkish delight for you. I've been learning backgammon for ten days. I'm very happy. See you soon. With (my) love.

Listening comprehension Guess who?

He was born on 8 January 1935 in Mississippi, in Tupel.
He made his first record in 1954.
He signed a contract with RCA in 1955.
He was on TV for the first time in 1956.
He did his military service in Germany in 1958.
He married Priscilla Beaulieu in 1967.
Lisa Marie was born in 1968.
He got divorced in 1973.
He gave 300 concerts between 1970–7.
He died on 16 August 1977 in Memphis, Tennessee.
He made more than 900 records.
He acted in more than 31 musicals.
He had three Grammy awards, 37 gold and 26 platinum records.
He was the king of rock'n'roll.

Reading comprehension Turkish history

The Turks came to Anatolia from Central Asia. Seljuk Turks entered Anatolia through Manzikert (Malazgirt) in 1071 and spread westward. Osman Bey got as far as Bursa. Later Bursa became the Ottomans' capital. In 1453 the Conqueror Sultan Mehmet took Constantinople and made it the Ottomans' capital. The Ottoman Empire extended as far as Vienna in the centre of Europe. The Ottomans built beautiful mosques, bridges and inns in Europe and Anatolia. After the First World War the British, French, Italian and Greeks invaded Turkey. Atatürk won the War of Independence. Turkey became a Republic. Ankara became the capital city. Atatürk became the first President of the Republic and carried out many reforms.

transcripts

This section contains the transcripts of all the listening exercises, and of the role-play exercises that are on the recording but not in the book.

Unit 1

Mini-test
1 Merhaba. 2 Hoşça kal. Hoşça kalın. 3 İyi geceler. 4 Nasılsınız? 5 Nasılsın? 6 Teşekkürler. Sağol. 7 See the **Alphabet and pronunciation** section in the **Introduction**. 8 See Unit 1, Numbers. 9 Ben [*your name*]. 10 İyiyim. Teşekkürler. Siz nasılsınız?

Role play
This exercise is not in the book.

Sema	Merhaba, Gökhan.
Gökhan	*Say 'hello, Sema'.*
	Merhaba, Sema.
Sema	Nasılsın?
Gökhan	*Say you are fine and ask how she is.*
	İyiyim, sen nasılsın?
Sema	Ben de iyiyim.
Gökhan	*Say 'goodbye'.*
	Hoşça kal.
Gülen	Hoşça kal.

Unit 2

Exercise 2
a Bira? b Çay? c Nescafé? d Ayran? e Şarap?

Exercise 3

a	çay	çaylar
b	rakı	rakılar
c	tost	tostlar
d	teşekkür	teşekkürler
e	bira	biralar
f	içecek	içecekler

Mini-test

1 Garson. 2 Bir şekerli kahve, lütfen *or* Bir şekersiz kahve, lütfen *or* Bir sade kahve, lütfen. 3 Sütlü Nescafé, lütfen. 4 Bir bardak çay, lütfen. 5 Bir bardak kırmızı ve bir bardak beyaz şarap, lütfen. 6 Çerez, lütfen. 7 Afiyet olsun. 8 Hesap, lütfen. 9 Üstü kalsın. 10 Elli, yetmiş, doksan, yüz.

Role play

This exercise is not in the book.

Waiter	Buyrun, efendim.
You	*Ask for a glass of tea.*
	Bir bardak çay, lütfen.
Waiter	Başka?
You	*Ask for a toasted cheese sandwich.*
	Bir peynirli tost, lütfen.
Waiter	Tabii, efendim.
You	*Thank him.*
	Teşekkürler.

Unit 3

Exercise 1

a İkiyüzkırkaltı elli otuzbeş. b İkiyüzaltmışiki sıfırbir otuzyedi. c Altıyüzondört onüç otuzüç. d Yediyüzonyedi yirmiiki yirmidört. e Sekizyüzdoksanaltı otuzaltı otuzaltı. f Üçyüzonbir kırksekiz elliyedi.

Number and letter dictation

This exercise is not in the book.

1 A 2 G 3 J 4 Ö 5 R 6 U 7 Ş 8 O 9 I 10 C 11 Ç 12 İ 13 K 14 S 15 Y 16 V 17 Ü 18 P 19 Ğ 20 E

Mini-test

1 Duşlu bir oda, lütfen. 2 Boş oda var mı? 3 Kahvaltı dahil mi? 4 ... nasıl yazılır? 5 Bu, şu, o. 6 Ben, sen, o, biz, siz, onlar.

Role play
This exercise is not in the book.

Receptionist	Hoş geldiniz.
You	*Reply to the receptionist's 'welcome' and ask if they have a vacant room.*
	Hoş bulduk. Boş oda var mı?
Receptionist	Evet, var.
You	*Say you want a single room.*
	Tek kişilik bir oda, lütfen.
Receptionist	Tabii.
You	*Ask if it has a shower.*
	Duş var mı?
Receptionist	Var, efendim. Kaç gece?
You	*Book the room for five days.*
	Beş gece.
Receptionist	Tabii, efendim. Pasaport, lütfen.
You	*Thank her.*
	Teşekkürler.

Unit 4

Mini-test
1 Bir kahve, tereyağı, ekmek, sosis ve yumurta, lütfen. 2 Balık tava ve yeşil salata, lütfen. 3 Bir büyük beyaz şarap, lütfen. 4 İki porsiyon köfte ve pilav, lütfen. 5 Bira soğuk mu?

Role play
This exercise is not in the book.

Waiter	Buyrun, efendim.
You	*Ask for a minced meat* pide *(Turkish pizza) and a* lahmacun *(savoury pancake).*
	Bir kıymalı pide ve bir lahmacun, lütfen.
Waiter	Tabii, efendim. İçecek?
You	*Ask for a yoghurt drink and a cola.*
	Bir ayran, bir kola, lütfen.

Unit 5

Exercise 5
a İstanbul'dan Ankara'ya 454 km. b İstanbul'dan Bodrum'a 815 km. c İstanbul'dan Çanakkale'ye 325 km. d İstanbul'dan

Safranbolu'ya 404 km. e İstanbul'dan Pamukkale'ye 666 km. f İstanbul'dan Marmaris'e 814 km. g İstanbul'dan Göreme'ye 750 km. h İstanbul'dan İzmir'e 565 km. i İstanbul'dan Trabzon'a 1,079 km. j İstanbul'dan Fethiye'ye 926 km.

Exercise 7

a Birinci gün: Marmaris'ten – Çiftlik'e. b İkinci gün: Çiftlik'ten – Bozukkale'ye. c Üçüncü gün: Bozukkale'den – Aktur'a ve Datça'ya. d Dördüncü gün: Datça'dan – Knidos'a. e Beşinci gün: Knidos'tan – Bodrum'a.

Mini-test

1 Afedersiniz, banka nerede acaba? 2 Afedersiniz, taksiler nerede acaba? 3 Düz gidin ve köşede sağa dönün, lütfen. 4 Müze ne zaman açık? 5 İki bilet, lütfen.

Role play

This exercise is not in the book.

You	*Ask politely where the museum is.*
	Afedersiniz, müze nerede acaba?
Passer-by	Düz gidin, sağda, PTT'den sonra.
You	*Thank him / her.*
	Çok teşekkür ederim.

Unit 6

1 a İzmir nerede? Batıda. b İstanbul nerede? Kuzey-batıda. c Ankara nerede? Ortada. d Van nerede? Doğuda. e Bodrum nerede? Güney-batıda. f Samsun nerede? Kuzeyde. g Mersin nerede? Güneyde. h Alanya nerede? Güneyde. i Marmaris nerede? Güney-batıda.

Mini-test

1 Yazın hiç yağmur yok. 2 İlkbaharda yağmur var / yağmurlu. 3 Temmuz şubattan (daha) sıcaktır. 4 En çok dans etmeyi (*to dance*) ve voleybolu seviyorum. 5 Bodrum'a hangi günler uçak var? 6 Bir meyveli dondurma, lütfen.

Role play

This exercise is not in the book.

You	*Ask what the weather is like in Alanya in July.*
	Temmuzda Alanya'da hava nasıl?
Clerk	Sıcak, yağmursuz. Hep güneşli.
You	*Ask if there are any flights to Alanya.*
	Alanya'ya uçak var mı?

Clerk	Evet, salı, perşembe ve cumartesi günleri.
You	*Ask if there is a seat available for (a place on) Thursday.*
	Perşembe için yer var mı?
Clerk	Evet, var. Kaç kişilik?
You	*Say 'for one person'.*
	Bir kişi için / Bir kişilik.

Unit 7

Exercise 4

a   Ben İstanbul'luyum.
    İstanbul'un neresinden?
    Ataköy.
b   Bu tatilde Türkiye'deyiz.
    Türkiye'nin neresinde?
    Güneyde, Alanya'da.
c   Bu Türkçe'de ne demek?
    Harita demek.
d   Bu İngilizce'de ne demek?
    Map demek.
e   Siz manken misiniz?
    Hayır, sekreterim. Ya siz?
    Ben öğrenciyim.

f   Ben 45 yaşındayım.
    Ben 23 yaşındayım.
g   Bu telefon numaram 595 33 22.
    Bu da benim telefon
    numaram 454 78 81.
    Teşekkürler.
h   Ben İngilizim.
    Gerçekten mi?
    Evet, Londra'lıyım.
i   Ben bekarım. Ya, siz?
    Ben evliyim. Eşim orada.
j   Tarkan Alman mı?
    Hayır, Türk.

Exercise 6

- Merhaba. Adım Bülent. Ben Türküm. Doktorum. İzmir'liyim.

- Manken. Amerikalı. Bekar. Adı Lucy. 24 yaşında.

- Trish Webb. Nerelisiniz Trish Hanım?
  İngilizim. Birmingham'lıyım.
  Evli misiniz?
  Hayır, bekarım.
  Öğretmensiniz, değil mi?
  Evet, öğretmenim.

- Phillipe. Fransız. Bekar. Futbolcu. 21 yaşında. Parisli.

- Merhaba. Adım Ülkü Gezer. Fotoğrafçıyım. Türküm. Evliyim. İstanbul'luyum. 43 yaşındayım.

- Merhaba, June Hanım.
  Merhaba.
  Sekreter misiniz?
  Hayır, hostesim.
  Amerikalı mısınız?
  Hayır, Avustralya'lıyım. Sydney'liyim.

Evli misiniz?
Evet, evliyim. Eşim Türk.

Mini-test

1 Amerikalı mısınız? (='Are you American?') 2 Kaç
yaşındasınız? 3 Milliyetiniz ne? 4 Evliyim. 5 Bekar mısınız?
6 Siz (Hanım. Bey); sen.

Role play

This exercise is not in the book.

Turk	Merhaba.
You	*Say 'hello'.*
	Merhaba.
Turk	Ben Türküm, siz Amerikalı mısınız?
You	*Say no, you're not American, you're English.*
	Hayır, Amerikalı değilim, İngilizim.
Turk	Aaa! Ben bekarım. Siz evlisiniz değil mi?
You	*Say yes, you're married to a Turk.*
	Evet, bir Türkle evliyim.
Turk	Gerçekten mi? Çok ilginç. Ben öğretmenim.
You	*Say you're an engineer.*
	Mühendisim.
Turk	Çok akıllısınız.
You	*Return the compliment. Say she's very clever too.*
	Siz de çok akıllısınız.

Unit 8

Exercise 2

Buyrun, efendim.
Bir pantolon bakıyorum.
Kaç beden?
40.
Buyrun, bu pantolon çok güzel.
Kahverengi bana yakışmıyor. Siyah veya gri var mı?
Buyrun bir siyah, bir gri. 40 beden.
Kaç lira?
80 milyon.
Denemek istiyorum, lütfen.
Tabii.

Mini-test

1 40 beden, mavi bir ceket, istiyorum, lütfen. 2 Naneli lokum,
lütfen. 3 Yarım kilo kuru yemiş, lütfen. 4 Bir paket kimyon,
lütfen. 5 Şarap içmiyorum. 6 41 numara, ayakkabı bakıyorum

/ istiyorum, lütfen. **7** Mavi pantalon, bakıyorum / Mavi pantalon, istiyorum, lütfen.

Role play

This exercise is not in the book.

Sales person	İyi günler. Buyrun, efendim.
You	*Say 'hello' and ask how much the leather jackets are.*
	Merhaba. Deri ceketler ne kadar?
Sales person	Kaç beden?
You	*Say 'size 40'.*
	40 beden.
Sales person	Ne renk?
You	*'Blue'.*
	Mavi.
Sales person	Sizin için 120 sterlin.
You	*Say 'It's too expensive.'*
	Çok pahalı.
Sales person	Pazarlık yapmıyoruz, ama sizin için 100 sterlin. Bu da son fiyat.
You	*Say 'OK, I'll buy it'.*
	Tamam, alıyorum.

Unit 9

Exercise 1

Yeşim	Bu akşam ne yapalım?
Ahmet	Tiyatroya gidelim.
Yeşim	Çok pahalı.
Ahmet	Sinemaya gidelim mi?
Yeşim	Sinemalar çok uzak.
Ahmet	Restorana gidelim.
Yeşim	Ben rejimdeyim.
Ahmet	Ne yapalım?
Yeşim	Televizyon seyredelim, mi?
Ahmet	Çok iyi fikir. Gazeteye bakalım neler var.

Exercise 2

4 ağustos pazartesi günü saat 8'de Banu'yla tiyatroya gidiyorum.
6 ağustos çarşamba günü saat bir buçukta Gonca'yla öğle yemeği yiyoruz.
8 ağustos cuma günü Yeşim ve Ahmet'le Boğaz gezisi yapıyoruz.
9 ağustos cumartesi günü saat ikida Çemberlitaş Hamamına gidiyorum.
10 ağustos pazar günü Vanessa ile Karagöz ve Hacivat'a gidiyoruz.

Exercise 4

a on iki otuz; yarım **b** on beş on beş; üçü çeyrek geçiyor **c** sekiz elli; dokuza on var **d** dört yirmi beş; dördü yirmi beş geçiyor **e** on sekiz kırkbeş; yediye çeyrek var **f** dokuz on; dokuzu on geçiyor **g** yirmi dört; gece yarısı – on iki **h** on on; onu on geçiyor **i** beş beş; beşi beş geçiyor **j** on üç iki; biri iki geçiyor

Mini-test

1 Tiyatroya gidelim mi, iyi bir oyun var. 2 İstanbul'a iki gidis dönüş bileti, lütfen. 3 Üçü çeyrek geçiyor. 4 Saat kaç? 5 Bu pazar için bir bilet, lütfen.

Role play

This exercise is not in the book.

Friend Bu akşam ne yapalım?
You *Say 'Let's go to a pub'.*
Hadi puba gidelim.
Friend Yarın çalışıyorum.
You *Say 'Shall we watch TV?'*
Televizyon seyredelim mi?
Friend Güzel program yok. Lokantaya gidelim mi?
You *Say 'It's a very good idea. Let's.'*
Çok iyi fikir. Hadi.

Unit 10

Guess who?

8 ocak 1935'te Mississippi, Tupel'de doğdu.
1954'te ilk kez plak yaptı.
1955'te RCA ile anlaştı.
1956'da ilk kez TV'ye çıktı.
1958'de askerliğini Almanya'da yaptı.
1967'de Priscilla Beaulieu ile evlendi.
1968'de Lisa Marie doğdu.
1973'te boşandı.
1970–77 arası 300 konser verdi.
16 ağostos 1977'de Tennessee Memphis'de öldü.
900'den fazla plak yaptı.
31'den fazla müzikalde oynadı.
3 Grammy ödülü, 37 altın, 26 platin plak ödülü aldı.
Rock'n'roll kralıydı.

Exercise 1

Happy holidaymaker

You   İyi günler.
Tourist İyi günler.
You   Tatiliniz nasıldı?
Tourist Çok iyiydi.
You   Hava nasıldı?
Tourist Her gün güneşliydi.
You   Otel nasıldı?
Tourist Çok rahattı, oda deniz manzaralıydı.
You   Yemekler nasıldı?
Tourist Yemekler harikaydı.

Unhappy holidaymaker

You   İyi günler.
Tourist İyi günler.
You   Tatiliniz nasıldı?
Tourist Çok kötüydü.
You   Hava nasıldı?
Tourist Çok rüzgarlı ve yağmurluydu.
You   Otel nasıldı?
Tourist Otel çok gürültülüydü.
You   Yemekler nasıldı?
Tourist Yemekler, berbattı, lezzetsizdi.

Mini-test

1 Tatilin(iz) nasıldı? 2 Berbattı. Herşey çok kötüydü.
3 Hamama gittim. 4 Çamur banyosu yapmadım. 5 Hiç deveye
bindin mi?

Role play

This exercise is not in the book.

Friend Dün ne yaptın?
You   *Say you went to the beach.*
            Plaja gittim.
Friend Deniz nasıldı? Burada yağmur yağdı.
You   *Say the weather and the sea were very good. Ask
            what he / she did.*
            Burada hava ve deniz çok güzeldi. Sen ne yaptın?
Friend Çalıştım.

key to the exercises

Unit 1
Dialogue 1
Hayır. Bey.

Dialogue 2
1 İyi. 2 İyi.

Dialogue 3
Çok güzel.

Dialogue 4
İyi.

Practice
1 a Merhaba. Selam. b Merhaba. Selam. İyi günler. c İyi günler. Günaydın. 2 İyi geceler. 3 Hoşça kal / Hoşça kalın. 4 Hoşça kal / Hoşça kalın / Güle güle. 5 a Merhaba b ben. 6 e, c, b, d, a, f. 7 a 5, b 10, c 1, d 9, e 3, f 7, g 4, h 2, i 6, j 8, k 0. 8 a yedi, b iki, c altı, d dokuz, e sekiz, f iki, g üç, h dokuz, i sekiz 10 merhaba, bir, nasılsın, hanım, bey, iki, sen, siz, iyiyim, on

Mini-test
1 Merhaba. 2 Hoşça kal. Hoşça kalın. 3 İyi geceler. 4 Nasılsınız? 5 Nasılsın? 6 Teşekkürler. Sağol. 7 See the **Alphabet and pronunciation** section in the **Introduction**. 8 See Unit 1, Numbers. 9 Ben [*your name*]. 10 İyiyim. Teşekkürler. Siz nasılsınız?

Unit 2 Drinks
Dialogue 1
1 Çay, Nescafé, su. 2 Sütlü.

Dialogue 2

1 Şekerli ve şekersiz (sade) / Çok güzel. 2 Evet, çok güzel.

Dialogue 3

1. Kırmızı. 2 Evet, beyaz peynir.

Practice

a çay, b kahve, c bira, d şarap, e rakı. 2 a Bira? b Çay?
c Nescafé? d Ayran? e Şarap? 3 a çaylar, b rakılar, c tostlar,
d teşekkürler, e biralar, f içecekler. 4 a yeşil, b turuncu, c gri,
d pembe, e mor. 6 a Yanlış, b Yanlış, c Doğru, d Doğru,
e Yanlış. 7 a 0, b 57, c 11, d 35, e 23, f 46, g 60.
8 Kahve, bira, süt, vişne suyu, şarap, ayran, rakı, çay, su

Mini-test

1 Garson. 2 Bir şekerli kahve, lütfen *or* Bir şekersiz kahve,
lütfen *or* Bir sade kahve, lütfen. 3 Sütlü Nescafé, lütfen. 4 Bir
bardak çay, lütfen. 5 Bir bardak kırmızı ve bir bardak beyaz
şarap, lütfen. 6 Çerez, lütfen. 7 Afiyet olsun. 8 Hesap, lütfen.
9 Üstü kalsın. 10 Elli, yetmiş, doksan, yüz.

Unit 3 Accommodation

Dialogue 1

1 Evet, var. 2 Yeşil Ev. 3 Y – e – ş – i – l E – v. 4 Otel.

Dialogue 2

1 Var. 2 İki tek yataklı, büyük ve güzel (balkonlu, deniz
manzaralı). 3 Üç. 4 Evet.

Dialogue 3

1 Evet, var. 2 Evet, var. 3 Elektrik, su, restoran, yüzme-
havuzu, plaj, duşlar, çocuk oyun parkı, ilk yardım, genel
telefon.

Dialogue 4

1 Evet, var. 2 Evet, var. 3 Ayşegül meşgul.

Practice

1 a İkiyüzkırkaltı elli otuzbeş. b İkiyüzaltmışiki sıfırbir
otuzyedi. c Altıyüzondört onüç otuzüç. d Yediyüzonyedi
yirmiiki yirmidört. e Sekizyüzdoksanaltı otuzaltı otuzaltı.
f Üçyüzonbir kırksekiz elliyedi. 2 a 531 b 444 c 6,755 d 1,001
e 3,033 f 916 g 7,814 h 4,000. 3 a v, b i, c vi, d ii, e iii, f iv.
4 a vii, b v, c iv, d i, e ii, f iii, g vi. 6 a ben, b sen, c o, d o, e o,
f biz, g siz, h onlar 7 otel, duş, anahtar, manzaralı, küvet,
yatak, balkonlu, oda, kahvaltı, pansiyon

Mini-test
1 Duşlu bir oda, lütfen. 2 Boş oda var mı? 3 Kahvaltı dahil
mi? 4 ... nasıl yazılır? 5 Bu, şu, o. 6 Ben, sen, o, biz, siz, onlar.

Unit 4 Eating out

Dialogue 1
1 Doğru. 2 Doğru. 3 Çok güzel. 4 Tereyağı, bal, marmelat,
reçel, peynir, zeytin, sosis, sucuk, salam, domates, salatalık,
biber, ekmek. 5 Evet, var. 6 Masada.

Dialogue 2
1 Doğru. 2 Doğru. 3 Evet. 4 Evet. 5 Hayır, lüfer ızgara.
6 Hayır, Asuman (Hanım) için.

Dialogue 3
1 Doğru. 2 Doğru. 3 İki porsiyon. 4 White bean salad. 5 Evet.

Practice
1 Çay, reçel, peynir, yumurta, zeytin, tereyağı, şeker. 2 a mi?
b mi? c mi? d mu? e mu? f mü? 3 a, d, b, e, c, f. 4 a çay b balık,
c salata, d ekmek. 5 a Evet, Istanbul'da. b Evet, soğuk. c Evet,
et. d Evet, ucuz. e Hayır, meyve. f Evet, lezzetli. g Hayır,
alkolsüz. h Evet, tatlı. i Hayır, yeşil. j Evet, taze. 6 a iv, b iii,
c vi, d ii, e i, f v.

Mini-test
1 Bir kahve, tereyağı, ekmek, sosis ve yumurta, lütfen. 2 Balık
tava ve yeşil salata, lütfen. 3 Bir büyük beyaz şarap, lütfen.
4 İki porsiyon köfte ve pilav, lütfen. 5 Bira soğuk mu?

Unit 5 Directions

Dialogue 1
1 Evet. 2 Hayır. 3 Evet.

Dialogue 2
1 9'dan 5'e kadar. 2 Topkapı'da. Düz gidin, işaretler var.

Dialogue 3
1 Evet, var. 2 Sahilde, merkezde.

Practice
1 a iii, b iv, c i, d ii. 2 a iii, b v, c ii, d iv, e i. 3 a Here you are.
b On me. c Do not disturb! d Excuse me. e I am sorry. f I do
not know. g Thanks. h Not at all. 4 a i / iii, b i / iii, c v, d vi,
e iv, f ii / iv. 5 a 454 km b 815 km c 325 km d 404 km

e 666 km f 814 km g 750 km h 565 km i 1,079 km j 926 km.
6 a Where is the information office? b Pass the traffic lights.
c Go straight ahead, take the first road on the right. d Go
straight ahead, on the left, at the corner. 7 a Marmaris'ten,
Çiftlik'e. b Çiftlik'ten, Bozukkale'ye. c Bozukkale'den, Aktur'a
ve Datça'ya. d Datça'dan, Knidos'a. e Knidos'tan, Bodrum'a.

Mini-test
1 Afedersiniz, banka nerede acaba? 2 Afedersiniz, taksiler
nerede acaba? 3 Düz gidin ve köşede sağa dönün, lütfen.
4 Müze ne zaman açık? 5 İki bilet, lütfen.

Unit 6 I like the weather here!

Dialogue 1
1 Güney. 2 Antalya. 3 Pazartesi, çarşamba, cuma, cumartesi,
pazar.

Dialogue 2
1 football, basketball, volleyball, tennis. 2 the sea, dancing, ice
cream, day trips. 3 Yağmursuz ve rüzgarsız güzel bir gün.
4 Evet, çok. 5 Beş çeşit.

Reading comprehension
1 Doğru. 2 Yanlış. 3 Doğru. 4 Yanlış. 5 Doğru. 6 Yanlış.

Practice
1 a Batıda. b Kuzey-batıda. c Ortada. d Doğuda. e Güney-
batıda. f Kuzeyde. g Güneyde. h Güneyde. i Güney-batıda.
2 a iv, b ii, c i, d iii, e vi, f viii, g v. 3 Dursun en kısa boylu.
4 a ağus_tos_ b _eylül_ c _ekim_ d _haziran_ e te_mmuz_ f şu_bat_ 6 hava,
sisli, yağmurlu, soğuk, sıcak, açık, karlı, bulutlu, güneşli,
rüzgarlı

Mini-test
1 Yazın hiç yağmur yok. 2 İlkbaharda yağmur var / yağmurlu.
3 Temmuz şubattan (daha) sıcaktır. 4 En çok dans etmeyi (*to
dance*) ve voleybolu seviyorum. 5 Bodrum'a hangi günler uçak
var? 6 Bir meyveli dondurma, lütfen.

Unit 7 Talking about oneself and describing people

Dialogue 1
1 Bonn. 2 Leeds. 3 İngiliz. 4 Türkçe, Almanca, Fransızca, İspanyolca, İtalyanca, Bulgarca. 5 Erkek.

Dialogue 2
1 Turkish. 2 Nobody. 3 İngiliz. 4 Öğrenci. 5 Ayda, doktor. 6 Evet. Cem uzun boylu, esmer, siyah saçlı, siyah gözlü, akıllı ve iyi bir insan.

Dialogue 3
1 İyi. 2 İyi.

Dialogue 4
1 İyi.

Practice
1 **a** Tarkan is a very handsome man. **b** Sezen Aksu is a very beautiful woman. **c** Are the teachers very clever? **d** You are a hard-working student. **e** Turkish is very interesting. **f** Turkey is both an historic and a modern country. **g** There are a lot of unemployed in Turkey. **h** Turkish is very easy. **i** English is a very rich language, isn't it? **j** German and French grammar are very difficult. 2 **a** A i, **b** E ii, **c** F vi, **d** G viii, **e** C iii, **f** H vii, **g** D v, **h** B iv. 3 **a** 3, **b** 4, **c** 8, **d** 1, **e** 7, **f** 9, **g** 2, **h** 5, **i** 6. 4 **a** x, **b** ix, **c** vi, **d** viii, **e** iii, **f** vii, **g** v, **h** ii, **i** i, **j** iv. 5 **a** i, **b** iii, **c** v, **d** vi, **e** vii, **f** viii, **g** ix, **h** x, **i** iv, **j** ii.

6

Name	Nationality	Job	Marital status	Age	Home town
Bülent	Turkish	doctor	____	____	Izmir
Lucy	American	model	single	24	___
Trish Webb	English	teacher	single	_	Birmingham
Phillipe	French	footballer	single	21	Paris
Ülkü Gezer	Turkish	photographer	married	43	Istanbul
June	Australian	air hostess	married	_	Sydney

Mini-test
1 Amerikalı mısınız? (= 'Are you American?') 2 Kaç yaşındasınız? 3 Milliyetiniz ne? 4 Evliyim. 5 Bekar mısınız? 6 Siz (Hanım, Bey); sen.

Unit 8 Shopping

Dialogue 1
1 Some shopping. 2 To the Grand Bazaar / Kapalı Çarşı.

Dialogue 2
1 Siyah. 2 Evet.

Dialogue 3
1 Laura. 2 Hayır, istemiyor. 3 Yarım kilo.

Dialogue 4
1 No. 2 No. 3 Dört kutu. 4 Hayır, yeni değil. 5 Evet, çok taze.

Dialogue 5
1 38 beden. 2 Hayır, yakışmıyor.

Practice
1

2 e, g, a, b, f, i, h, c, d, k, j. **3 Food:** Türk kahvesi; çerez; bal; elma çay; lokum; fıstık; incir; **Clothes:** T-shirt; bluz; ceket; ayakkabı; pantalon; çanta; **Presents:** padişah macunu; CD; kaset; halı; kilim; cüzdan; baharat **4** lokum, baharat, deri, ayakkabı, fıstık, şapka, kilim, bluz, pantalon, ceket

Mini-test
1 40 beden, mavi bir ceket, istiyorum, lütfen. 2 Naneli lokum, lütfen. 3 Yarım kilo kuru yemiş, lütfen. 4 Bir paket kimyon, lütfen. 5 Şarap içmiyorum. 6 41 numara, ayakkabı bakıyorum / istiyorum, lütfen. 7 Mavi pantalon, bakıyorum / Mavi pantalon, istiyorum, lütfen.

Unit 9 Where shall we go?

Dialogue 1

1 They're going to go to the theatre. 2 They look at the Kenter Theatre's schedule. 3 Tiyatroya. 4 Kenterler'e. 5 Film. 6 Yarımda. 7 (*Personal response.*)

Dialogue 2

1 No, there aren't. 2 Two. 3 Yanlış. 4 Doğru. 5 Yanlış. 6 Doğru. 7 (*Personal response.*)

Dialogue 3

1 To the cinema. 2 No. 3 *Vampirler, Şaban, Hamam.* 4 *Hamam'a.* 5 Yedide. 6 Otobüsle gidiyorlar. 7 Araba bozuk ve otobüs daha ucuz. 8 (*Personal response.*)

Dialogue 4

1 To Taksim. 2 Return. 3 Evet. 4 Evet. 5 Hayır.

Practice

1 a ii, iii, iv, vi. b To watch TV.

c Yeşim	Bu akşam ne yapalım?
Ahmet	Tiyatroya gidelim.
Yeşim	Çok pahalı.
Ahmet	Sinemaya gidelim mi?
Yeşim	Sinemalar çok uzak.
Ahmet	Restorana gidelim.
Yeşim	Ben rejimdeyim.
Ahmet	Ne yapalım?
Yeşim	Televizyon seyredelim, mi?
Ahmet	Çok iyi fikir. Gazeteye bakalım neler var.

2 Yes, Tuesday and Thursday 3 a ii, b iv, c i, d iii. 4 a on iki otuz; yarım b on beş on beş; üçü çeyrek geçiyor c sekiz elli; dokuza on var d dört yirmi beş; dördü yirmi beş geçiyor e on sekiz kırkbeş; yediye çeyrek var f dokuz on; dokuzu on geçiyor g yirmi dört; gece yarısı – on iki h on on; onu on geçiyor i beş sıfır beş; beşi beş geçiyor j on üç sıfır iki; biri iki geçiyor. 5 a İkiyi beş geçiyor. b Üçe yirmi beş kala. c Dördü çeyrek geçe. d Yediye çeyrek var. e Yarımda. f Sekize on var. g Saat yediyi yirmibeş geçe. h On biri çeyrek geçiyor. i Ona çeyrek var. j Dokuzu beş geçe. 6 a Sinemada. b Tiyatroda. c İşte. d Parkta. e Otobüste. f Trende. g Vapurda. h Dolmuşta. i Uçakta. j Durakta. k Otelde. 7 a iii, i, ii, iv. b iv, ii, i, iii *or* iv, iii, ii, i 8 a From Eminönü. b Three boats at 10.35, 12.00 and 13.35. c At six places; the 7th place is the last stop. d For 2–3

hours. **9 a** ii, **b** iv, **c** iii, **d** vi, **e** v, **f** i, **g** viii, **h** ix, **i** x, **j** xi, **k** xii, **l** vii. **10** Let's love 'green' and protect the forests; *or* We should love 'green' and protect the forests.

Mini-test
1 Tiyatroya gidelim mi, iyi bir oyun var. **2** İstanbul'a iki gidis dönüş bileti, lütfen. **3** Üçü çeyrek geçiyor. **4** Saat kaç? **5** Bu pazar için bir bilet, lütfen.

Unit 10 How was it?

Dialogue 1
1 Harikaydı. **2** Sakin, masmavi ve ılıktı. **3** Yüzdüler, kürek çektiler ve kumlarda yürüdüler. **4** Rahattı, oda deniz manzaralıydı, servis iyiydi (ve yemekler harikaydı). **5** Harikaydı.

Dialogue 2
1 İyi değildi. Önce çok sıcaktı, sonra rüzgarlı ve yağmurluydu. **2** Berbattı. Deniz soğuk ve çok dalgalıydı. **3** Hayır, hiç iyi değildi. Gürültülüydü, hiç manzara yoktu, yatak sertti ve duş bozuktu. **4** Yemekler berbattı, lezzetsizdi. Sebze ve meyveler taze değildi.

Reading comprehension The postcard
1 Hayır, içmedi. **2** Hayır, İstanbul'da. **3** Hayır, henüz gezmedi.

Listening comprehension Guess who?
1 Elvis Presley. **2** Evet, yaptı. **3** Priscilla Beaulieu ile evlendi. **4** Evet, yakışıklıydı. **5** Şarkıcı ve aktördü. **6** Evet, çok ünlüydü. **7** (*Personal response.*)

Reading comprehension Turkish history
1 Sultan Mehmet took Constantinople and made it the capital of the Ottoman Empire. **2** The Ottomans built beautiful mosques, bridges and inns in Europe and Anatolia. **3** Atatürk won the War of Independence, he became the first President of the Republic, and he carried out many reforms.

Practice
1 Happy holidaymaker: **a** i, **b** ii, **c** vi, **d** vii, **e** ix; unhappy holidaymaker: **a** x, **b** viii, **c** v, **d** iv, **e** iii. **2 i** b, **ii** d, **iii** c, **iv** a.

	ben	sen	o
doğmak	doğdum	doğdun	doğdu
anlaşmak	anlaştım	anlaştın	anlaştı
TV'ye çıkmak	çıktım	çıktın	çıktı
plak yapmak	yaptım	yaptın	yaptı
evlenmek	evlendim	evlendin	evlendi
boşanmak	boşandım	boşandın	boşandı
konser vermek	verdim	verdin	verdi
oynamak	oynadım	oynadın	oynadı
ödül almak	aldım	aldın	aldı
ölmek	öldüm	öldün	öldü

4 1 geldi(ler) 2 girdi 3 yayıldı 4 geldi 5 oldu 6 aldı 7 yaptı
8 durdu(lar) 9 yaptı(lar) 10 etti(ler) 11 kazandı 12 oldu 13 oldu
14 oldu 15 yaptı. 5 Hiç tavla oydadın mı? / Hiç nargile içtin
mi? / Hiç simit yedin mi? / Hiç deveye bindin mi? / Hiç çamur
banyosu yaptın mı? / Hiç Ayasofya'yı gezdin mi? / Hiç
hamama gittin mi? / Hiç Mavi Yolculuk yaptın mı? / Hiç Türk
Kahvesi içtin mi? / Hiç Karagöz ve Hacivat'ı seyrettin mi? / Hiç
rakı içtin mi? 7 harika, bozuk, berbat, rahat, iyi, sert,
gürültülü, masmavi, pahalı, dalgalı

Mini-test
1 Tatilin(iz) nasıldı? 2 Berbattı. Herşey çok kötüydü.
3 Hamama gittim. 4 Çamur banyosu yapmadım. 5 Hiç deveye
bindin mi?

1 The alphabet

The English alphabet has 26 letters: *Aa*, *Bb*, *Cc*, *Dd*, *Ee*, *Ff*, *Gg*, *Hh*, *Ii*, *Jj*, *Kk*, *Ll*, *Mm*, *Nn*, *Oo*, *Pp*, *Qq*, *Rr*, *Ss*, *Tt*, *Uu*, *Vv*, *Ww*, *Xx*, *Yy*, *Zz*.

The Turkish alphabet has 29 letters: **Aa, Bb, Cc, Çç, Dd, Ee, Ff, Gg, Ğğ, Hh, Iı, İi, Jj, Kk, Ll, Mm, Nn, Oo, Öö, Pp, Rr, Ss, Şş, Tt, Uu, Üü, Vv, Yy, Zz.**

Letters are divided into two groups called vowels and consonants.

For more information see Unit 3.

1.1 Vowels

The English vowels are: *a*, *e*, *i*, *o*, *u*.

The Turkish vowels are: **a, ı, o, u, e, i, ö, ü.**

1.2 Vowel harmony

Vowel harmony is used to harmonize Turkish vowels correctly. Any vowels added to a word have to rhyme or 'harmonize' with the previous vowel in the word.

See Units 2, 4 and 5 and the **Appendix**.

1.3 Consonants

The English consonants are: *b*, *c*, *d*, *f*, *g*, *h*, *j*, *k*, *l*, *m*, *n*, *p*, *q*, *r*, *s*, *t*, *v*, *w*, *x*, *y*, *z*.

The Turkish consonants are: **b, c, ç, d, f, g, ğ, h, j, k, l, m, n, p, r, s, ş, t, v, y, z.**

For more information see Units 3–5.

2 Adjectives

An adjective is a word that describes a noun or a pronoun, e.g. *good, beautiful, young*. Turkish adjectives, like other Turkish words, take endings.

2.1 Comparatives

Comparatives are used when comparing people, animals, objects or groups. English uses the ending *-er* or *more* to compare: *Turkey is warmer than England*. In Turkish **daha** is used for comparisons, e.g. **Türkiye İngiltere'den daha güneşli.** Not all English adjectives follow the rule but almost all Turkish adjectives do.

For more information see Unit 6.

2.2 Superlatives

Superlatives are used when comparing more than one person, animal, object or group. In English, *-est* is added to the end of the object or *most* is placed before the adjective, e.g. *prettiest, most expensive*. In Turkish, **en** means *the most (-est)*. The word **en** is put before the adjective: **Ağustos en sıcak ay. En güneşli yer.**

For more information see Unit 6.

3 Articles

A, an, the are called articles. In general, articles are not used in Turkish. As is mentioned in Unit 2 the equivalent of *a / an* is either **bir** or nothing. English uses *the* to talk about specific items. Likewise in Turkish, you use the **-i** ending if the direct object is a specific item. At this stage, don't worry about getting these endings right. People will understand you even if you do not use them. Just try to notice them when you hear or see them.

For more information see Units 2–5.

4 Nouns

Words which name things (objects, ideas, people or places) are called nouns. *Woman, cinema, money* and *water* are all examples of nouns.

English nouns are divided into countable and uncountable nouns. Countable nouns can be singular or plural but uncountable nouns cannot. *Water, money* and *sugar* are examples of uncountable nouns. In English, you usually add *-s* or -*es* to the end of countable nouns. In English, some nouns are always plural, e.g. *jeans*, *trousers*, *glasses*. In Turkish, all nouns can be either singular or plural.

Use the singular noun if there is just one and add the plural ending if there is more than one. In Turkish, all nouns (names of things, opinions and feelings, etc.) can be made plural by adding **-ler** or **-lar**. Unlike English, however, there are no exceptions in Turkish. In Turkish most greetings and wishes are in plural, e.g. **İyi akşamlar**. *Good evening*.

For more information see Unit 2.

4.1 Proper nouns

These are words that have their own special name, such as people's names, city names, countries, etc. All proper nouns begin with a capital letter, e.g. *Vanessa*, *Ayşegül*, *Paris*, *Istanbul*, *Turkey*.

4.2 Pronouns

Pronouns are short words, which are used instead of nouns to avoid repetition, e.g. *I*, *you*, *he*, *she*, *it*, *we*, *they*. The Turkish pronouns are: **ben, sen, o, biz, siz, onlar**.

For more information see Unit 3.

5 Negative

Negative means *not*, e.g. *He is not English*. In Turkish **değil** is used to make a word or phrase negative, e.g. **O İngiliz değil**. For more information see Unit 1.

To tell people not to do things, add **-me** or **-ma** to the end of the main part of the verb, e.g. **Git*me***. *Do **not** go*. For more information see Unit 6.

6 Word order

Although Turkish word order is relatively free and flexible, it is best to follow the main principle that verbs go at the end of the sentence. The basic word order is Subject – Object – Verb (SOV) (see Unit 7).

6.1 Subject

The subject in the sentence is the person or thing performing the action.

Example: The <u>cat</u> chased the mouse.

6.2 Object

The object of the sentence is the person or thing having the action done to it.

Example: The cat chased the <u>mouse</u>.

6.3 Verbs

Verbs are often called 'doing words'; they tell us what is happening, e.g. *go, do, walk, swim*. Remember *am, are, is, was* and *were* are verbs (verb *to be*). Verbs change according to who does something and / or when something happens. When you look up a word in an English dictionary (for the dictionary form) you see the main part of the verb with *to* in front of it, e.g. *to mean, to ask*.

6.3.1 Infinitive

The dictionary form of Turkish verbs is the stem plus the ending **-mek** or **-mak**. Dictionary forms are sometimes called 'the infinitive'. Sometimes the dictionary form is used as it stands, and sometimes you use it to make the correct form of the verb.

6.3.2 Tense

The main tenses of verbs are present, past and future. Time is split into past, present and future. We can alter verbs (doing words) to show when the action is taking place.

In English, *I walk* is in the simple present tense and *I am walking* is in the continuous present tense. In Turkish, the **-er** ending is used in the present tense and **-iyor** is used for the present continuous tense.

In English we add *-ed* to most verbs to show the past tense, e.g. *walked, talked.* Not all English verbs follow this rule so there are a lot of irregular past tense verbs, e.g. *go* → *went, swim* → *swam.* To make a past tense in Turkish you almost always add the **-di** ending (according to vowel harmony), to the main part of the verb.

appendix: vowel harmony

e-type endings

For e-type endings, use this rule:

e	goes after	e, i, ö, ü
a	goes after	a, ı, o, u

The following are e-type endings:

-ler	plural
-de	'at', 'on', 'in'
-mek	'to' (infinitive)
-e	'to', 'for'
-den	'from'
-me	'not'
-ce	makes a language word from a nationality word (adj.)
-elim	'let's'
-le	'by', 'with', 'using'

i-type endings

For i-type endings, use this rule:

i	goes after	e, i
ı	goes after	a, ı
ü	goes after	ö, ü
u	goes after	o, u

Here are some common i-type endings:

-mı?	question word
-ı	Turkish equivalent of 'the'
-cı	denotes a person or occupation
-dır	'is': very formal usage
-lı	'with', 'containing', 'from'
-iyor	-ing (present tense)
-dı	past tense
-lık	'-ness'
-siz	'without'

ABD *USA*
acaba *I wonder, please*
acıkmak *to get hungry*
acıktım *I'm hungry*
açık *open / light colour*
açmak *to open, to switch on*
ad *name*
ada *island*
adres *address*
adım *my name* (first name)
adınız *your name*
afedersiniz *excuse me*
afiyet olsun *enjoy your drinks!
/ enjoy your meal!*
ağır *heavy*
ağrımak *to ache*
ağrıyor *aching*
ağustos *August*
Akdeniz *Mediterranean*
akıl *intelligence*
akıllı *clever, intelligent*
akılsız *stupid, silly*
akşam *evening*
akşamlar *evenings*
aktör *actor*
aldı *conquered, took*
alfabe *alphabet*
alış veriş *shopping*
almak *to buy, to take*
Alman *German* (people)
Almanca *German* (language)

Almanya *Germany*
alo *hello* (on the phone)
altın *gold*
ama *but*
Amerika *America*
Amerikalı *American* (people)
Anadolu *Anatolia*
anahtar *key*
anlamak *to understand*
anlaşmak *to sign a contract*
anne *mother*
annemler *my parents* (lit. *my
mothers*)
ara sıra *sometimes*
araba *car*
aralık *December*
aramak *to call*
arası *between*
arasında *in between*
arayayım *let me call (I'll call)*
arkadaş *friend*
arkadaşım *my friend*
arı *bee*
arı soktu *a bee has stung me*
askerliğini yaptı *did his
military service*
askerlik *military service*
aspirin *aspirin*
Asya *Asia*
Asyalı *Asian*
atmak *to put*

Avrupa *Europe*
Avrupalı *European*
Avustralyalı *Australia*
ayakkabı *shoes*
ayakkabıcı *shoe shop*
Ayasofya *St. Sophia*
ayırtmak *to book, to reserve*
ayran *yoghurt-based drink*
ayrı *separate*

baba *father*
baharat *spices*
bahşiş *tip*
bakalım *let's have a look*
bakkal *grocer / grocer's*
baklava *Turkish dessert*
bakmak *to look*
bal *honey*
balık *fish*
balıkçı *fishing / fisherman*
balkon *balcony*
balkonlu *with a balcony*
bana *me, for me*
bana da *for me too*
bana Yasemin deyin *call me
  Yasemin*
banka *bank*
banyo *bathroom*
barbunya *red mullet*
bardak *glass*
basketbol *basketball*
baş *head*
Başbakan *Prime Minister*
başım ağrıyor *I have a headache*
başka *what else*
başka bir şey *anything else*
başkent *capital*
bekar *single*
Belçika *Belgium*
Belçikalı *Belgian* (people)
ben *I*
ben de *me too, I too*
bence *in my opinion*
benden *on me*

benim *my, it's me*
benim için *for me*
berbat *terrible*
bey *Mr* (after first names only)
beyaz *white*
beyazlı *dressed in white*
bıçak *knife*
bırak! *leave!*
bırakmak *to leave*
biber *pepper*
bikini *bikini*
bile *even*
bilet *ticket*
bilet gişesi *ticket office*
bilgisayar *computer*
biliyor *he / she knows*
biliyorum *I know*
bilmek *to know*
bilmiyorum *I don't know*
bina *building*
bir buçukta *at half past one*
bira *beer*
biraz *a little*
birbirimiz *each other*
birinci *first*
Birinci Dünya Savaşı *First
  World War*
biz *we*
bluz *blouse*
boş *vacant / empty*
boşanmak *to get divorced*
bozmak *to break*
bozuk *change* (money); *broken,
  out of order*
bölge *region*
börek *pastry*
börekçi *pastry shop*
Britanya *Britain*
bu *this*
buçuk *it's half past*
buçukta *it's (at) half past*
buğulama *steamed*
bugün *today*
Bulgar *Bulgarian* (people)

Bulgarca   *Bulgarian* (language)
Bulgaristan   *Bulgaria* (country)
bunlar   *these are*
burada   *here*
burası   *here, this place*
buraya   *here* (shows movement)
Bursa'ya kadar   *as far as Bursa*
butik   *boutique*
buyrun   *yes, I'm listening to you; here you are / do come in*
buyrun, efendim?   *how can I help you, sir / madam?*
büfe   *food stall*
büro   *office*
bütün   *all*
büyük   *big*

cadde   *street*
cami   *mosque*
canım   *my dear*
canlı   *alive, live*
ceket   *jacket*
cevap   *answer*
cevap vermek   *to answer*
cezve   *Turkish coffee maker*
cız bız   *sizzling / fried*
ciddi   *serious*
cuma   *Friday*
cumartesi   *Saturday*
Cumhurbaşkanı   *President*
cumhuriyet   *republic*
cüzdan   *wallet, purse*

çadır   *tent*
çalmak   *to ring*
çalışkan   *hard working*
çamur   *mud*
çamur banyosu   *mud bath*
çanta   *bag*
çarşamba   *Wednesday*
çatal   *fork*
çay   *tea*
çek   *pull*
çekmek   *to pull*

çerez   *snacks*
çeşit   *kind, type*
çeşitli   *various*
çeyrek   *a quarter*
çık!   *come out / get out*
çıkmak   *to come out / go up*
çiçek   *flower*
çift   *a pair*
çikolatalı   *chocolate flavoured / with chocolate*
çizme   *boots*
çoban-salatası   *mixed salad*
çocuk   *child*
çocuklar   *children*
çok   *very*

da   *also*
dağ   *mountain*
daha   *more (-er)*
dahil   *included*
dahil mi?   *is it included?*
dakika   *minutes*
dalgalı   *rough*
dalmak   *to dive*
-dan, (-den) sonra   *after*
danışma   *information*
dans   *dance*
dantel   *lace*
-de   *at, on, in*
değil   *not*
değil mi?   *Isn't it?*
değişik   *different*
-den beri   *since*
-den -e   kadar   *from ... to ....*
-den önce   *before ....*
-den sonra   *after .....*
denemek   *to try on*
deniz   *sea*
deniz kenarları   *seaside*
deri   *leather*
ders   *lesson, class*
dersten sonra   *after the class*
devamlı   *continuous*
deve   *camel*

devrimler *reforms*
dikkat et! *watch out! pay attention! be careful!*
dil *language, tongue*
dilimlenmiş *sliced*
doğmak *to be born*
doğru *right / true*
doğum tarihi *date of birth*
doğum yeri *place of birth*
doktor *doctor*
dolmuş *sharing taxi*
dolmuşla *by sharing taxi*
domates *tomatoes*
don *frost*
dondurma *ice cream*
dön *turn!*
döner *doner*
dönmek *to turn / return / rotate* (takes -e or -a ending e.g. **sola dön**)
dönüş *return*
durak *stop, bus stop*
durdular *stopped*
durmak *to stop*
duş *shower*
dut *mulberry*
dün *yesterday*
dünya *world*
dürüst *honest*
düz *straight*

-e, -a kadar *as far as*
eczane *chemist's*
efendim *sir or madam, pardon*
efendim? *pardon?*
Ege *Aegean*
ekim *October*
ekmek *bread*
elbise *dress*
eldiven *gloves*
elektrik *electricity*
elma *apple*
elma çay *apple tea*
emekli *retired*

en *the most (-est *)*
en sıcak *hottest*
en yakın *nearest*
erkek *man*
eski *old*
esmer *dark / olive skinned*
eşim *my wife / my husband (my partner)*
et *meat*
etek *skirt*
etli *with meat*
etsiz *without meat*
ev *house, home*
eve *to the house*
evet *yes*
evlenmek *to get married to*
evli *married*
eylül *September*

fal bakmak *to read fortunes*
falan *roughly, or so, and such like*
farklı *different*
farklıyız *we are different*
Fatih Sultan Mehmet *Sultan Mehmet the Conqueror*
fındık *hazelnuts*
fırın *bakery / oven*
fıstık *nuts*
fıstıklı *nutty*
fikir *idea*
film *film*
fiyatlar *prices*
Fransa *France*
Fransız *French* (people)
Fransızca *French* (language)
futbol *football*

galiba *I think*
garson *waiter / waitress*
gazete *newspaper*
gece *night*
gece yarısı *midnight*
geç *cross!*

geç kaldım *I'm late*
geçen *last*
geçiyor (-i) *past*
geçmek *to cross*
geldim *I've come / I came*
gelecek *next, coming*
gelmek *to come*
genel telefon *a public phone*
genellikle *generally*
gerçekten *really*
gerek *necessary*
gezi *trip / journey*
gezmek *travel / trip*
gidelim mi? *shall we go?*
gidin *go (please)*
gir *enter!*
girdi *entered*
giriş *entrance*
girmek *to enter*
git *go!*
gitmek *to go*
gökkuşağı *rainbow*
gölge *shade*
gömlek *shirt*
görmek (-i) *to see*
görüşmek(ile) *to see each other*
görüşürüz *see you*
gözlük *glasses*
gramlık *per gram*
gri *grey*
gül *rose*
güle güle *goodbye* (reply to
  hoşça kal *or* hoşça kalın)
güle güle kullanın! *enjoy using
  it*
gümrük *customs*
gün *day*
güneş *sun*
güneşli *sunny*
güney *south*
günlük *daily (day)*
gürültü *noise*
gürültülüydü *it was noisy*
güzel *beautiful, nice*

hadi *let's / come on*
hadi, arayalım *let's call*
hafta *week*
hafta sonu *weekend*
haklısınız *you are right*
halı *carpet*
Hamam *Turkish bath* (Hamam
  is also the name of a Turkish
  film)
hangi? *which?*
Hanım *Miss / Mrs / Ms* (after
  first names only)
harabe *ruin*
harem *harem*
harika *wonderful*
harikaydı *It was wonderful*
harita *map*
hastahane *hospital*
hava *air / weather*
havaalanı *airport*
havlu *towel*
hayır *no*
haziran *June*
hediye *present*
hediyelik şeyler *things for
  presents*
hem … hem *both … and*
hemen *straight away*
henüz *only, yet*
hep *all*
hepsi bu kadar *that's all*
her *every*
her zaman *always*
hergün *everyday*
herşey *everything*
herşey herşey *absolutely
  everything*
hesap *the bill*
hızlı *fast*
hiç *(not) at all, never*
Hindistan *India*
Hintçe *Indian / Hindu*
Hintli *Indian* (people)
hisar *fortress*

hostes   *air hostess*
hoş   *nice, pleasant*
hoş bulduk   the standard reply
  to **hoş geldiniz** *or* **hoş geldin**
hoş geldiniz   *welcome*
hoşça kalın   *goodbye*

ılık   *warm*
ılıktı   *it was warm*
ışıklar   *lights*
ızgara   *grilled*

içecek   *drink*
içecekleriniz   *your drinks*
içmek   *to drink*
iken   *while / when*
iklim   *climate*
ilginç   *interesting*
ilk   *first*
ilk yardım   *first aid post*
ilkbahar   *spring*
incir   *fig*
İngiliz   *English* (people)
İngilizce   *English* (language)
İngiltere   *England*
insan   *person*
inşaat   *building site*
iskele   *port*
İspanya   *Spain*
İspanyol   *Spanish* (people)
İspanyolca   *Spanish* (language)
istasyon   *station*
istemek   *to want*
istiyorum   *I want / I would like*
iş   *work, job*
işaret   *sign*
işgal etmek   *to occupy*
işgal ettiler   *occupied*
işsiz   *unemployed*
işte   *here, here it is, there*
it   *push*
İtalyan   *Italian* (people)
İtalyanca   *Italian* (language)
itmek   *to push*
iyi   *good*

iyi akşamlar   *good evening*
iyi geceler   *good night*
iyiyim   *I am fine*
iyiyiz   *we are well*

Japon   *Japanese* (people)
Japonca   *Japanese* (language)
Japonya   *Japan*

kabak   *courgette, pumpkin*
kaç beden?   *what size?*
kaç gün?   *how many days?*
kaç günlük?   *for how many days?*
kaç kişi?   *how many people?*
kaç kişilik?   *for how many*
  people?
kaç lira?   *how much? (lira)*
kaç saat?   *how many hours?*
kadın   *woman*
kahvaltı   *breakfast*
kahvaltıda   *at breakfast*
kahve(ler)   *coffee(s)*
kahveli   *coffee flavoured*
kahverengi   *brown*
kalacak yer listesi   *lists of*
  accommodation
kalkan   *turbot*
kalkış   *leaving*
kalkmak   *to get up, to leave*
kalmak   *to stay*
kamp   *campsite*
Kanada   *Canada*
Kanadalı   *Canadian* (people)
Kapalı Çarşı   *Grand Bazaar*
kapatmak   *to close, to switch*
  off, to cover
kar   *snow*
Karadeniz   *The Black Sea*
kardeş   *sibling*
kardeşim   *my sister / my brother*
karışık   *mixed*
karışık meyve   *mixed fruit*
karpuz   *watermelon*
karşı   *opposite*
kart   *card*

kartla *by card* (see **ile**)
kaset *tape*
kasım *November*
kayısı *apricot*
kazak *jumper*
kazandı *won*
kazanmak *to win*
kemer *belt*
kere *times*
kervansaraylar *caravanserai*
  (inns with large courtyards)
keyif *pleasure, delight, joy,*
  enjoyment
keyifli *joyous, pleasurable,*
  enjoyable
kez *time*
Kıbrıs *Cyprus*
Kıbrıslı *Cypriot*
kır *countryside / wild*
kır çiçekleri *wild flowers*
kırmızı *red*
kış *winter*
kızarmış *toasted*
kızımız *our daughter*
kilim *woven rug*
kilise *church*
kilo *kg*
kiloluk *for a kilo*
kimyon *cumin*
kiremit *brick*
kiremitte *baked / roast on a tile*
  in the oven
kişi *person*
kolay *easy*
komedi *comedy*
komik *funny*
konser *concert*
kontrol *check in*
korku *horror*
korumak *to protect*
koymak *to put, to put ... on*
köfte *Turkish meatballs*
köfteci *restaurant serving*
  Turkish meatballs
köftelik *for meatballs*

köpek *dog*
köprü *bridge*
köşe *corner*
kötü *bad*
kötüydü *it was bad*
köy *village*
kral *king*
kredi *credit*
kredi kartı *credit card*
kuaför *hairdresser*
kum *sand*
kumlar *sands*
kurak *dry*
Kurtuluş Savaşı *War of*
  Independence
kuru yemiş *dried fruit*
kutu *box*
küçük *small*
küpe *earrings*
kürek çekmek *to row a boat*
küvet *bath*

lahmacun *savoury pancake*
levrek *bass*
lezzetli *tasty*
likör *liquor*
liman *port*
limonata *still lemonade*
limonlu *lemon flavoured*
liste *list*
lokanta *restaurant*
lokum *Turkish delight*
lokumcu *Turkish delight shop*
lüfer *blue fish*
lüks *luxury*
lütfen *please*

maalesef *unfortunately* (a polite
  remark)
magazin *magazine*
Malazgirt *town in south-east*
  Turkey
manken *model*
manzara *view*
manzaralı *with a view*

Marmara   *Marmara* (the sea and region)
mart   *March*
masa   *table*
masada   *on the table*
masmavi   *very intense blue*
mavi   *blue*
Mavi Yolculuk   *Blue Cruise*
mayıs   *May*
mayo   *swimming costume*
memnun oldum   *I'm glad*
merhaba / selam   *hello / hi*
merkez   *centre*
mermer   *marble*
meslek   *job, profession*
meşgul   *busy*
meşgulüm   *I am busy*
meşgulüz   *we are busy*
mevsim   *season*
meyve   *fruit*
meyveli   *fruit flavoured / with fruit*
meze   *starter*
Mısır   *Egypt, corn*
Mısırlı   *Egyptian* (people)
milliyet   *nationality*
modern   *modern*
mor   *purple*
mönü   *menu*
muhteşem   *great*
mutlu   *happy*
mutsuz   *unhappy*
mühendis   *engineer*
müze   *museum*
müzik   *music*
müzikal   *musical*

nane   *mint*
naneli   *peppermint flavoured*
nargile   *hookah*
nasıl?   *how?*
nasıl yazılır?   *how do you spell it?*
nasılsın? (sen)   *how are you?*

nasılsınız? (siz)   *how are you?*
ne?   *what?*
ne oynuyor?   *what's on?*
ne yapalım?   *what shall we do?*
neden?   *why?*
neler?   *what are there?*
nerede?   *where?*
nereler?   *what places?*
nerelisin?   *where are you from?*
neresi?   *where / which place?*
nereye?   *where to?* (shows movement)
nereye gidelim?   *where shall we go?*
Nescafé   *instant coffee*
neyle (ne ile)?   *by what? / with what? / how* (see ile)
niçin? (ne için)   *why?*
nisan   *April*
nişanlı   *engaged*
nişanlın   *your fiancé*
numara   *number*

o   *that* (referring to something relatively far away)
o   *he / she / it*
ocak   *January*
oda   *room*
okumak   *to read*
olarak   *as*
onlar   *they*
orada   *there*
orman   *forest*
orta   *medium*
Orta Asya   *Central Asia*
Orta Avrupa   *Central Europe*
orta boy   *medium sized*
ortada   *in the middle, centre*
ortalama   *average*
Osman Bey   *Osman* (the head of the Ottoman clan)
Osmanlılar   *Ottomans*
otel   *hotel*
otobüs   *bus*

otobüs bileti *bus ticket*
otobüs durağı *bus stop*
otobüsle *by bus*
otoyol *motorway*
oynamak *to act, to play*
oyun parkı *play area*

ödemek *to pay*
ödül *award*
öğlen *noon*
öğrenci *student*
öğrenmek *to learn*
öğretmek *to teach*
öğretmen *teacher*
ölmek *to die*
önce *at first, ago*
önümüzde *in front of us*
özel *special*
özellikle *especially*
özür dilemek *to apologize*
özür dilerim *I'm sorry*

padişah macunu *aphrodisiacs*
pahalı *expensive*
paket *packet, parcel*
pansiyon *guest house*
pantalon *trousers*
park *park*
parti *party*
pasaport *passport*
pasaport numarası *passport number*
pasta *cake*
pastahane *cake shop*
patates *potatoes*
patlıcan *aubergine, egg plant*
pazar *Sunday*
pazarlık *bargain*
pazarlık yapmak *to bargain, haggle*
pazartesi *Monday*
pembe *pink*
pencere *window*
perde *curtain*

perşembe *Thursday*
peynir *cheese*
pide *Turkish pizza*
pideci *a Turkish pizza restaurant*
pilav *cooked rice*
pilavlı *with cooked rice*
piliç *chicken*
piyaz *white bean salad*
plaj *beach*
plak *record*
platin *platinum*
popüler *popular*
porsiyon *portion*
posta *post*
profesör *professor*
program *programme*

rafadan *soft-boiled egg*
rahat *comfortable*
rahatsız etmeyin! *do not disturb!*
rakı *aniseed-flavoured spirit*
reçel *jam*
rejimdeyim *I'm on a diet*
renk *colour*
renkler *colours*
resepsiyon memuru *receptionist*
restoran *restaurant*
rica ederim *not at all*
roka *rocket leaves*
Rus *Russian* (people)
Rusça *Russian* (language)
Rusya *Russia*
rüya *dream*
rüzgar *wind*
rüzgarlı *windy*
rüzgarsız *without wind / windless*

saat *time, hour or clock*
saat kaç? *what time is it?*
saat kaçta? *at what time?*
sabah *morning*

saç   *hair*
sade   *plain / vanilla flavour,*
  without sugar
sağ   *right*
sağ olun / sağol   *thanks*
  (showing respect and gratitude)
sağda   *on the right*
sahil   *coast*
sakin   *calm*
salam   *salami*
salatalık   *cucumber*
salı   *Tuesday*
samimi   *friendly*
sana   *for you, to you*
sandal   *rowing boat*
sandalet   *sandals*
saniye   *seconds*
saray   *palace*
sarı   *yellow*
satmak   *to sell*
sebze   *vegetables*
sekreter   *secretary*
Selçuk Türkleri   *Seljuk Turks*
sen   *you* (singular)
serin   *cool*
sert   *hard*
servis   *service*
sevgi   *affection, love*
sevgili   *beloved, dear*
seviyorlar   *they love*
seviyorum   *I like*
seviyoruz   *we like / love*
sevmek   *to love*
sevmiyoruz   *we do not like /*
  love
seyahat   *travel*
seyahat acentası   *travel agency*
seyretmek   *watch*
sıcak   *hot*
sıkıcı   *boring*
sıkılmak   *to be bored*
simit   *bread* (in the shape of a
  big ring)
sinema   *cinema*

sır   *secret*
sırrımız   *our secret*
sis   *fog*
sisli   *foggy*
siyah   *black*
siyah gözlü   *dark-brown eyed*
  (lit. *black eyed*)
siyah saçlı   *black haired*
siz / sen   *you* (see Unit 1)
sizin   *your*
sizin için   *for you*
sokmak   *to sting*
sol   *left*
sonbahar   *autumn / fall*
sonra   *than, later*
sor   *ask!*
sormak   *to ask*
sosis   *sausage*
soyad   *surname*
soyadım   *my surname*
sözlük   *dictionary*
spor   *sport*
su   *water*
sucuk   *spicy Turkish sausage*
sudan ucuz   *very cheap*
sumak   *sumac*
susadım   *I'm thirsty*
sür   *drive*
sürmek   *to drive*
süt   *milk*
sütlü   *with milk*

şampuan   *shampoo*
şans   *chance / luck*
şapka   *hat*
şarap   *wine*
şaraprengi   *wine-coloured*
şarkıcı   *singer*
şeker   *sugar*
şekerli   *with sugar, sweet*
şekersiz   *without sugar*
şemsiye   *umbrella*
şimdi   *now*
şiş kebap   *shish kebab*

şişe   *bottle*
şoför   *driver*
şu   *that is, that*
şubat   *February*
şunlar   *these*
şurada   *there*
şurası   *there, that place*

tabii   *of course*
takım elbise   *suit*
taksi   *taxi*
Taksim   *Taksim Square in Istanbul*
tam   *right, exactly, adult, full price*
tamam   *OK*
tarif   *recipe*
tarih   *history, date*
tarihi   *ancient, historic*
taşımak   *to carry*
tatil   *holiday*
tatiliniz   *your holiday*
tatiller   *holidays*
tatlı   *dessert*
tatlı yiyelim, tatlı konuşalım   *let's eat sweet, speak sweet* (a common saying when offering sweet)
tava   *fried*
tavla   *backgammon*
taze   *fresh*
tek kişilik   *single room*
tek yataklı   *single bed*
tekrar   *again*
telefon numaraları   *telephone numbers*
tembel   *lazy*
temiz   *clean*
temizlik yapmak   *to do cleaning*
temmuz   *July*
tenis   *tennis*
tereyağı   *butter*
teşekkür(ler)   *thanks*
tık tık   *knock knock*

tiyatro   *theatre*
Topkapı Müzesi   *Topkapı Museum*
tost (peynirli tost)   *toasted sandwich (toasted cheese sandwich)*
tren   *train*
turist   *tourist*
turizm   *tourism*
tüm   *all*
turkuaz mavi   *turquoise*
turuncu   *orange*
tuvalet   *toilet*
tuz   *salt*
tür   *kind*
Türk   *Turkish* (people)
Türk kahvesi   *Turkish coffee*
Türkçe   *Turkish* (language)
Türkiye   *Turkey*
TV'ye çıkmak   *to be on TV*

ucuz   *cheap*
uçak   *aeroplane*
uzak   *far*
uzun boylu   *tall / long*
uzundur   *it is long*

ülke   *country*
üniversite   *university*
ünlü   *famous*
üstü kalsın   *keep the change*
üzüm   *grapes*

valiz   *suitcase*
vapur   *boat*
var   *there is / are*
varış   *arrival, arriving*
varmak (-e)   *to arrive*
ve   *and*
vermek   *to give*
veya   *or*
vişne suyu   *sour cherry juice*
voleybol   *volleyball*

ya siz? / ya sen? *and you?*
yaşındayım *I'm x years old*
yağıyor *it's raining*
yağmak *to rain*
yağmur *rain*
yağmurlu *rainy*
yağmursuz *without rain / rainless*
yakın *near*
yakında *soon*
yakışklı *handsome*
yakışmak *to suit*
yalı *old wooden villa*
yanlış *wrong / false*
yapmak *to do*
yararlı *good for you*
yarım *half, half past twelve*
yarın *tomorrow*
yasak *forbidden*
yasaktır *it is forbidden*
yasaktır *forbidden*
yaş *age*
yaşlı *aged*
yatak *bed, mattress*
yavaş *slowly*
yavrum *my child* (shows affection)
yaya *pedestrian*
yayılmak *to spread*

yaz *summer*
yemek yemek *to eat food*
yer *place, seat*
yerken *while eating*
yeşil *green*
Yeşil Ev *Green House*
yok *there is none / we haven't got any*
yol *road*
yolcu *traveller*
yolcu vapuru *passenger boat*
yolculuk *journey*
yolumu kaybettim *I'm lost*
yorgun *tired*
yorgunum *I'm tired*
yoruldum *I'm tired*
yumurta *egg*
yüksek *high, loud*
yürümek *to walk*
yürüyerek *on foot*
yüzmek *to swim*
yüzme-havuzu *swimming pool*
yüzük *ring*

zaman *time*
zengin *rich*
zeytin *olives*
zeytinyağlı *cooked with olive oil*
ziyaret *visit*

English–Turkish vocabulary

absolutely everything *herşey*
herşey
ache, to *ağrımak*
aching *ağrıyor*
act, to *oynamak*
actor *aktör*
address *adres*
Aegean *Ege*
aeroplane *uçak*
affection *sevgi*
after *-dan, (-den) sonra*
after the class *dersten sonra*
again *tekrar*
age *yaş*
aged *yaşlı*
ago *önce*
air, weather *hava*
air hostess *hostes*
airport *havaalanı*
alive, live *canlı*
all *bütün, hep, tüm*
alphabet *alfabe*
also *da / de*
always *her zaman*
America *Amerika*
American (people) *Amerikalı*
Anatolia *Anadolu*
ancient, historic *tarihi*
and *ve*
and you? *ya siz? / ya sen?*
answer *cevap*

answer (to) *cevap vermek*
anything else *başka bir şey*
aphrodisiacs *padişah macunu*
apologize, to *özür dilemek*
apple *elma*
apple tea *elma çay*
apricot *kayısı*
April *nisan*
arrival, arriving *varış*
arrive, to *varmak (-e)*
as *olarak*
as far as; – Bursa *-e, -a kadar;*
Bursa'ya kadar
Asia *Asya*
Asian *Asyalı*
ask *sor*
ask, to *sormak*
aspirin *aspirin*
at *-de / -da*
at first *önce*
aubergine *patlıcan*
August *ağustos*
Australia *Avustralyalı*
autumn *sonbahar*
average *ortalama*
award *ödül*

backgammon *tavla*
bad *kötü*
bag *çanta*
bakery (oven) *fırın*

balcony; with a – *balkon; balkonlu*

bank *banka*

bargain *pazarlık*

bargain (to) (haggle) *pazarlık yapmak*

basketball *basketbol*

bass *levrek*

bath *küvet*

bath, bathroom *banyo*

beach *plaj*

beautiful *güzel*

bed, mattress *yatak*

bee; a – has stung me *arı; arı soktu*

beer *bira*

before ... *-den önce*

Belgium *Belçika*

Belgian (people) *Belçikalı*

beloved *sevgili*

belt *kemer*

between *arası*

big *büyük*

bikini *bikini*

bill *hesap*

black; – haired; the – Sea *siyah; siyah saçlı; Karadeniz*

blouse *bluz*

blue *mavi*; very intense – *masmavi*

blue fish *lüfer*

Blue Cruise *Mavi Yolculuk*

boat; passenger – *vapur; yolcu vapuru*

book (to) *ayırmak*

boots *çizme*

bored (to be) *sıkılmak*

boring *sıkıcı*

born (to be) *doğmak*

both ... and *hem ... hem*

bottle *şişe*

boutique *butik*

box *kutu*

bread *ekmek*

break (to) *bozmak*

breakfast *kahvaltı*

brick *kiremit, tuğla*

bridge *köprü*

Britain *Britanya*

brother (my) *kardeşim*

brown *kahverengi*

building *bina*

building site *inşaat*

Bulgaria (country) *Bulgaristan*

Bulgarian (language) *Bulgarca*

Bulgarian (people) *Bulgar*

bus; by –; – stop; – ticket *otobüs; otobüsle; otobüs durağı; otobus bileti*

busy; I'm busy *meşgul; işim var, meşgulüm*

but *ama*

butter *tereyağ*

cake; — shop *pasta; pastahane*

call (to) (i.e. on the telephone) *aramak; arayayım*; call me Yasemin *bana Yasemin deyin*

calm *sakin*

camel *deve*

campsite *kamp*

Canada *Kanada*

Canadian (people) *Kanadalı*

capital *başkent*

car *araba*

caravanserai *kervansaray*

card; by – *kart; kartla*

carpet *halı*

carry (to) *taşımak*

Central Asia *Orta Asya*

Central Europe *Orta Avrupa*

centre *merkez*; in the – *ortada*

chance *şans*

change; keep the – *bozuk para; üstü kalsın*

cheap *ucuz*

check in *kontrol*

cheese *peynir*

chemist's *eczane*

chicken *piliç*

child; my – *çocuk; yavrum*

chocolate flavoured / with
chocolate *çikolatalı*

church *kilise*

cinema *sinema*

class *ders*

clean *temiz*

clever *akıllı*

climate *iklim*

clock *saat*

coast *sahil*

close (to) *kapatmak*

coffee; – flavoured *kahve;*
kahveli

colour *renk*

come, to *gelmek*

come on *hadi*

come out (to) *çıkmak*

comedy *komedi*

comfortable *rahat*

coming *gelecek*

computer *bilgisayar*

concert *konser*

conquered *aldı*

continuous *devamlı*

cooked with olive oil *zeytinyağlı*

cool *serin*

corner *köşe*

country *ülke*

countryside *kır*

courgette *kabak*

cover (to) *kapatmak*

credit; – card *kredi, kredi kartı*

cross (to) *geçmek*

cross *geç*

cucumber *salatalık*

cumin *kimyon*

curtain *perde*

customs *gümrük*

Cypriot *Kıbrıslı*

Cyprus *Kıbrıs*

daily (day) *günlük*

dance *dans*

dark-brown eyed (lit. black eyed)
siyah gözlü

dark / olive skinned *esmer*

date of birth *doğum tarihi*

daughter; our – *kızımız*

day *gün*

dear; my – *sevgili; canım*

December *aralık*

dessert *tatlı*

dictionary *sözlük*

die (to) *ölmek*

diet; I'm on a – *rejim;*
rejimdeyim

different *değişik, farklı*

disturb; do not – *rahatsız;*
rahatsız etmeyin

dive (to) *dalmak*

do (to); cleaning *yapmak;*
temizlik yapmak

doctor *doktor*

dog *köpek*

doner *döner*

dream *rüya*

dress *elbise*

dressed in white *beyazlı*

dried fruit *kuru yemiş*

drink *içecek*

drink (to) *içmek*

drive *sür*

drive (to) *sürmek*

driver *şoför*

dry *kurak*

each other *birbirimiz*

earrings *küpe*

easy *kolay*

eat food (to) *yemek yemek*

egg; soft-boiled – *yumurta;*
rafadan

Egypt *Mısır*

Egyptian (people) *Mısırlı*

electricity *elektrik*

empty *boş*

engaged *nişanlı*

engineer *mühendis*

England *İngiltere*

English (language) *İngilizce*
English (people) *İngiliz*
enjoy (to); – using it; – your
  drinks; – your meal *güle güle
  kullanın; afiyet olsun*
enjoyable *keyifli*
enter (to) *girmek*
entrance *giriş*
especially *özellikle*
Europe *Avrupa*
European *Avrupalı*
even *bile*
evening *akşam*
every; – day; – thing *her;
  hergün; herşey*
excuse me *afedersiniz*
expensive *pahalı*

famous *ünlü*
far *uzak*
fast *hızlı*
father *baba*
February *şubat*
fiancé (your) *nişanlın*
fig *incir*
film *film*
fine; I'm – *iyi; iyiyim*
first *birinci*
first; – aid post *ilk; ilk yardım*
First World War *Birinci Dünya
  Savaşı*
fish *balık*
fisherman *balıkçı*
fishing *balıkçılık*
flower *çiçek*
fog *sis*
foggy *sisli*
foodstall *büfe*
foot; on – *yürüyerek*
football *futbol*
forbidden *yasak, yasaktır*
forest *orman*
fork *çatal*
fortress *hisar*
France *Fransa*

French (language) *Fransızca*
French (people) *Fransız*
fresh *taze*
Friday *cuma*
fried *tava, kızarmış*
friend; my – *arkadaş; arkadaşım*
friendly *samimi*
from ... to ... *-den -e kadar*
frost *don*
fruit; – flavoured / with –
  meyve, yemiş; meyveli
funny *komik*

generally *genellikle*
German (language) *Almanca*
German (people) *Alman*
Germany *Almanya*
get out *çık*
get up (to) *kalkmak*
give (to) *vermek*
glad; I'm – *memnun; memnun
  oldum*
glass *bardak*
glasses (spectacles) *gözlük*
gloves *eldiven*
go (to); please – *gitmek; gidin*
gold *altın*
good; – evening; – for you; –
  night *iyi; iyi akşamlar; yararlı;
  iyi geceler*
goodbye *hoşça kalın; güle güle*
  (reply to **hoşça kalın**)
Grand Bazaar *Kapalı Çarşı* (see
  Unit 8)
grapes *üzüm*
great *muhteşem*
green; – house *yeşil; yeşil ev*
grey *gri*
grilled *ızgara*
grocer / grocer's *bakkal*
guest house *pansiyon*

hair *saç*
hairdresser *kuaför*
half, half past twelve *yarım*

handsome *yakışıklı*
happy *mutlu*
hard; – working *sert, zor;*
  çalışkan
harem *harem*
hat *şapka*
hazelnuts *fındık*
he *o*
head; I have a –ache *baş; başım*
  ağrıyor
heavy *ağır*
hello; – (on the phone)
  merhaba; alo
here; – (shows movement); – you
  are; – it is; – this place *burada;*
  buraya; buyurun; işte; burası
hi *selam*
history *tarih*
holiday *tatil*
home *ev*
honest *dürüst*
honey *bal*
hookah *nargile*
horror *korku*
hospital *hastahane*
hot *sıcak*
hotel *otel*
hottest *en sıcak*
hour *saat*
house *ev*
how?; – (by –); – are you? – are
  you? … – can I help you
  sir/madam?; – do you spell it?; –
  many days?; – many hours?; –
  many people?; – much (lira)?
  nasıl?; neyle (ne ile), nasıl; (see
  ile); nasılsın? (sen); nasılsınız
  (siz); buyrun, efendim; nasıl
  yazılır?; kaç gün?; kaç saat?; kaç
  kişi; kaç lira?
hungry *aç*
hungry (to get) *acıkmak*

I *ben*
ice cream *dondurma*

idea *fikir*
in; – between; – front of us *-de;*
  arasında; önümüzde
include; is it included? *dahil;*
  dahil mi?
India *Hindistan*
Indian (people) *Hintli*
Indian / Hindu *Hintçe*
information *danışma*
instant coffee *Nescafé*
intelligence *akıl*
intelligent *akıllı*
interesting *ilginç*
island *ada*
isn't it? *değil mi?*
it *o*
Italian *İtalyanca*

jacket *ceket*
jam *reçel*
January *ocak*
Japan *Japonya*
Japanese (language) *Japonca*
Japanese (people) *Japon*
job, profession *meslek, iş*
journey *yolculuk*
joyous *keyifli*
July *temmuz*
jumper *kazak*
June *haziran*

keep the change *üstü kalsın*
key *anahtar*
kind *tür*
kind, type *çeşit*
king *kral*
knife *bıçak*
knock knock *tık tık*
know (to) *bilmek*

lace *dantel*
language *dil*
last *geçen*
late; I'm – *geç; geç kaldım*
later, than *sonra*

lazy *tembel*
leather *deri*
leave *bırak*
leave (to) *bırakmak*
leaving *kalkış*
left *sol*
lemon flavoured *limonlu*
lemonade (still) *limonata*
lesson *ders*
light (colour) *açık*
lights *ışıklar*
like (to) *sevmek*
liquor *likör*
list; lists of accommodation *liste; kalacak yer listesi*
little (a) *biraz*
long *uzun*
look (to) *bakmak*
lost; I'm – *kayıp; yolumu kaybettim*
loud *yüksek*
love (to) *sevmek*
luck *şans*
luxury *lüks*

magazine *magazin*
map *harita*
marble *mermer*
March *mart*
married; to get – to *evli; evlenmek*
mattress, bed *yatak*
May *mayıs*
me, for –; on –; – too *bana; benim için; benden; ben de*
meat; with –; without – *et; etli; etsiz*
Mediterranean *Akdeniz*
medium; – sized *orta; orta boy*
men *erkek*
menu *mönü*
middle; in the – *ortada*
midnight *gece yarısı*
military service *askerlik*
milk; with – *süt; sütlü*

mint *nane*
minutes *dakika*
Miss / Mrs / Ms (after first names only) *Hanım*
mixed; – fruit; – salad *karışık; karışık meyve; çoban-salatası*
model *manken*
modern *modern*
Monday *pazartesi*
more (comparative) *daha*
morning *sabah*
mosque *cami*
most (the) *en*
mother *anne*
motorway *otoyol*
mountain *dağ*
Mr (after first names only) *bey*
mud; – bath *çamur; çamur banyosu*
mulberry *dut*
museum *müze*
music *müzik*
musical *müzikal*
my, it's me *benim*

name *ad*
nationality *milliyet*
near *yakın*
nearest *en yakın*
necessary *gerek*
never *hiç*
newspaper *gazete*
next *gelecek*
nice *hoş*
night *gece*
no *hayır*
noise *gürültü*
noon *öğlen*
not; not at all *değil; rica ederim*
November *kasım*
now *şimdi*
number *numara*
nuts *fıstık*
nutty *fıstıkı*

occupy (to)   *işgal etmek*
October   *ekim*
office   *büro*
OK   *tamam*
old; – wooden villa   *eski; yalı*
olives; – skinned   *zeytin; esmer*
on; – foot; – me; – the right; – the table   *yürüyerek; benden; sağda; masada*
only   *henüz*
open   *açık*
open (to)   *açmak*
opinion; in my –   *fikir; bence*
opposite   *karşı*
or   *veya*
orange   *turuncu*
Ottomans   *Osmanlılar*
oven   *fırın*

packet   *paket*
pair   *çift*
palace   *saray*
pardon?   *efendim?*
parents, my – (lit. my mothers)   *annemler*
park   *park*
party   *parti*
passport; – number   *pasaport; pasaport numarası*
past   *geçiyor (-i)*
pastry; – shop   *börek; börekçi*
pay (to); – attention   *ödemek; dikkat et*
pedestrian   *yaya*
people   *kişi, insanlar*
pepper   *biber*
peppermint flavoured   *naneli*
person   *insan*
person   *kişi*
pink   *pembe*
place; – of birth   *yer; doğum yeri*
plain / vanilla flavour   *sade*
platinum   *platin*
play area   *oyun parkı*
please   *lütfen*

pleasant   *hoş*
pleasure   *keyif*
popular   *popüler*
port   *iskele*
port   *liman*
portion   *porsiyon*
post   *posta*
potatoes   *patates*
present   *hediye*
President   *Cumhurbaşkanı*
prices   *fiyatlar*
Prime Minister   *Başbakan*
profession, job   *meslek*
professor   *profesör*
programme   *program*
protect (to)   *korumak*
public phone   *genel telefon*
pull (to)   *çekmek*
purple   *mor*
purse / wallet   *cüzdan*
push   *it*
push (to)   *itmek*
put (to); to – ... on   *atmak; koymak*

quarter   *çeyrek*

rain; without –   *yağmur; yağmursuz*
rain (to)   *yağmak*
rainbow   *gökkuşağı*
rainy   *yağmurlu*
read (to); to – fortunes   *okumak; fal bakmak*
really   *gerçekten*
receptionist   *resepsiyon memuru*
recipe   *tarif*
record   *plak*
red; – mullet   *kırmızı; barbunya*
reforms   *devrimler*
region   *bölge*
republic   *cumhuriyet*
reserve (to)   *ayırmak*
restaurant   *lokanta; restoran*

retired *emekli*
return *dönüş*
rice (cooked); with cooked –
  pilav; pilavlı
rich *zengin*
right; on the –; – (exactly); –
  (true); you are – *sağ; sağda;*
  tam; doğru, haklısınız
ring *yüzük*
ring (to) *çalmak*
road *yol*
rocket leaves *roka*
room *oda*
rose *gül*
rough *dalgalı*
roughly *falan*
row a boat (to) *kürek çekmek*
rowing boat *sandal*
ruin *harabe*
Russia *Rusya*
Russian (language) *Rusça*
Russian (people) *Rus*

salad *salata*
salami *salam*
salt *tuz*
sand *kum*
sandals *sandalet*
sands *kumlar*
Saturday *cumartesi*
sausage *sosis*
sea *deniz*
seaside *deniz kenarları*
season *mevsim*
seat *yer*
seconds *saniye*
secret *sır*
see (to); to – each other *görmek;*
  görüşmek
secretary *sekreter*
Seljuk Turks *Selçuk Türkleri*
sell (to) *satmak*
separate *ayrı*
September *eylül*
serious *ciddi*

service *servis*
shade *gölge*
shampoo *şampuan*
she *o*
shirt *gömlek*
shish kebab *şiş kebap*
shoes; – shop *ayakkabı;*
  ayakkabıcı
shopping *alış veriş*
shower *duş*
sibling *kardeş*
sign *işaret*
sign a contract (to) *anlaşmak*
since 1777 *1777'den beri*
singer *şarkıcı*
single; – bed; – ticket *bekar; tek*
  yataklı; tek kişilik
sister (my) *kiz kardeşim*
size *beden, numara*
sizzling *cız bız*
skirt *etek*
sliced *dilimlenmiş*
slowly *yavaş*
small *küçük*
snacks *çerez*
snow *kar*
sometimes *ara sıra*
soon *yakında*
sorry (to be) *özür dilerim*
south *güney*
Spain *İspanya*
Spanish (language) *İspanyolca*
Spanish (people) *İspanyol*
special *özel*
spices *baharat*
sport *spor*
spread (to) *yayılmak*
spring *ilkbahar*
starter *meze*
station *istasyon*
stay (to) *kalmak*
steamed *buğulama*
sting (to) *sokmak*
stop (to) *durmak*
stop, bus – *durak*

straight; – away *düz; hemen*
street *cadde*
student *öğrenci*
stupid *akılsız*
sugar; with –; without – *şeker;*
  şekerli; sade
suit *takım elbise*
suit (to) *yakışmak*
suitcase *valiz*
sumac *sumak*
summer *yaz*
sun *güneş*
Sunday *pazar*
sunny *güneşli*
surname; my – *soyad; soyadım*
swim (to) *yüzmek*
swimming costume *mayo*
swimming pool *yüzme-havuzu*
switch off (to) *kapatmak*

table; on the – *masa; masada*
take (to) *almak*
tall *uzun boylu*
tape *kaset*
tasty *lezzetli*
taxi *taksi*
tea *çay*
teach (to) *öğretmek*
teacher *öğretmen*
telephone numbers *telefon*
  numaraları
tennis *tenis*
tent *çadır*
terrible *berbat*
than *sonra*
thanks; – (showing respect and
  gratitude) *teşekkür(ler); sağ*
  olun
that (referring to something
  relatively far way); – is; that's all
  o; şu; hepsi bu kadar
theatre *tiyatro*
there *orada*
there; – is none; – is / are; – (that
  place) *şurada; yok; var; şurası*

these; – are *şunlar; bunlar*
they *onlar*
think (to); I – *düşünmek; galiba*
thirsty (to be); I'm thirsty
  susamak; susadım
this *bu*
Thursday *perşembe*
ticket; – office *bilet; bilet gişesi*
time *kez*
time *zaman*
time (hour); at what –? *saat;*
  saat kaçta?
times *kere*
tip *bahşiş*
tired *yorgun*
toast (to) *kızarmış*
toasted sandwich (toasted cheese
  sandwich) *tost (peynirli tost)*
today *bugün*
toilet *tuvalet; 00*
tomatoes *domates*
tomorrow *yarın*
took, conquered *aldı*
tourism *turizm*
tourist *turist*
towel *havlu*
train *tren*
travel; – agency *seyahat; seyahat*
  acentası
travel (to) *gezmek*
traveller *yolcu*
trip (journey) *gezi*
trousers *pantalon*
true *doğru*
try on (to) *denemek*
Tuesday *salı*
turbot *kalkan*
Turkey *Türkiye*
Turkish (language) *Türkçe*
Turkish (people); – Bath; – coffee; –
  coffee maker; – delight; – delight
  shop; – meatballs; – restaurant; –
  pizza *Türk; Hamam; Türk*
  kahvesi; cezve; lokum; lokumcu;
  köfte; köfteci; pide

Turkish pizza restaurant *pideci*
turn *dön*
turn (to) *dönmek*
turquoise *turkuaz mavi*
TV (to be on) *TVye çıkmak*

umbrella *şemsiye*
understand (to) *anlamak*
unemployed *işsiz*
unfortunately (a polite remark)
 maalesef
unhappy *mutsuz*
university *üniversite*
USA *ABD*

vacant *boş*
various *çeşitli*
vegetables *sebze*
very *çok*
view; with a – *manzara; manzaralı*
village *köy*
visit *ziyaret*
volleyball *voleybol*

waiter / waitress *garson*
walk (to) *yürümek*
wallet *cüzdan*
want (to) *istemek*
War of Independence *Kurtuluş Savaşı*
warm *ılık*
watch (to) *seyretmek*
watch out! *dikkat et!*
water *su*
watermelon *karpuz*
we *biz*
weather *hava*
Wednesday *çarşamba*
week *hafta*
weekend *hafta sonu*

welcome *hoş geldiniz*
what?; – are there?; – else; – places?; – shall we do?; – size?; – time is it? *ne?; neler var?; başka ne?; nereler?; ne yapalım?; kaç beden?; saat kaç?*
where?; – are you from?; – shall we go?; – (shows movement); – (which place)? *nereye?; neresi?; nerelisin?; nereye gidelim?; nerede?;*
which? *hangi?*
while *-iken*
white; – bean salad *beyaz; piyaz*
why? *niçin? (ne için); neden?*
wife (my) *eşim; karım*
wild; – countryside; – flowers *kır; kır çiçekleri*
win (to) *kazanmak*
wind; without – *rüzgar; rüzgarsız*
window *pencere*
windy *rüzgarlı*
wine *şarap*
wine (colour) *şaraprengi*
winter *kış*
woman *kadın*
wonderful *harika*
work (job) *iş*
world *dünya*
woven rug *kilim*
wrong *yanlış*

yellow *sarı*
yes *evet*
yesterday *dün*
yet *henüz*
you; for –; to – *siz / sen; sana; senin için*
your *sizin*

The numbers refer to the units where the information is to be found.

accommodation 3
adjectives 6, 7
alphabet practice 3
asking questions 2, 3, 4, 7

ben, benim 7
ben, sen, o, biz, siz onlar 3
bir 2

capital letters 6
colours 2
commands and instructions 5
comparisons 6
connecting *y* 5, 9
countries 7

daha 6
dates 6
days of the week 6
-de, -da 4, 5
değil 1
-den, -dan 5
descriptions 7, 10
-dı, -di, -du, -dü 10
-dır, -dir, -dur, -dür 6
direct object 5
directions 5
'don't' 6

-e, -a 5
en 6
experiences 10

greetings 1, 7

'I, you, he, she, it, we, you, they' 3
ile 9
-iyor 8

jobs and professions 7

kaç? 3

-ler, -lar 2
-lı, -li, -lu, -lü 6, 7
likes and dislikes 6

making questions with *mı?, mi?, mu?, mü?* 4
-me, -ma 6
-mı, -mi, -mu, -mü 4
months 6

names 1, 7
nationalities 7
numbers 1, 2, 3

offering, accepting, refusing 9
ordering drinks 2
ordering meals 4

pairs 8
past tense 10
personal pronouns 3
plurals 2
present tense 8

seasons 6
sen/siz 1
shopping 8
-sız, -siz, -suz, -süz 6
suggestions 9

telephone calls 3
telephone numbers 3

telling the time 9
'the' 5
time expressions 10
'to be' 7
transport 9

var 2, 9
verbs, dictionary forms 5
vowel harmony 2, 4, 5, 7,
    Appendix

weather 6
word endings 6, 7
word order 5, 7

yemek yemek 6
yok 2